Unbelievable!
A Working Country Life

Unbelievable!

A Working Country Life

The story of **Martin Aris**:
farmer, river keeper and mischief-maker

Victoria Walsh

Chalk Stream Books

This book portrays actual events from the life of Martin Aris, and is as truthful as the passing of time and Martin's memory permits. I have corrected some obvious inaccuracies but allowed some mild ones to stand, where they do not affect another identifiable individual. All persons mentioned in the book are actual individuals, but some names have been changed or anonymised to respect their privacy. Neither Victoria nor Martin intend to cause any offence through the book or its marketing: this is just a frank account of a working country life.

To Martin, with thanks for your hard work and spectacular stories — you're unbelievable!

You don' wan' a lot in life when you've got the country like this!

Martin Aris

Contents

Part One: Spring

Part Two: Summer

Foreword

I've known Martin Aris for a long while, and it seems to me that the saying "Still waters run deep" sums him and the river under his care up.

You need to read carefully. Martin is a man who carries a wealth of knowledge that is camouflaged by his distinct Cotswolds-Wiltshire burr and manner of speaking. For a while, when you first read his words, you think he is just talking, but when you tune in to his nuances of language the knowledge he imparts will open your eyes to that very special world, the countryside of the Avon Valley, which he has inhabited for most of his life.

River keepers are a breed apart, and Martin is an exemplar of their type. He is knowledgeable, thoughtful, kind and helpful. But a day on a river is more than the fishing. It is about seeing nature in a different way. Sometimes that is not easy to see, but if you let Martin be your guide through the pages of this wonderful book, I promise you'll appreciate better the glories of the English countryside and a life well spent.

Simon Cooper — Nether Wallop Mill, March 2023

Simon Cooper is a fly fisher and Founder and Managing Director of Fishing Breaks (fishingbreaks.co.uk). He is the author of several books, including Life of a Chalkstream *and* The Otters' Tale.

10% of the profit from Unbelievable! will be donated to **The Angling Trust**. The Angling Trust is a not-for-profit organisation, representing anglers, and fighting for fish, fishing and the environment. We love the river here at The Mill, so we're very happy to donate to the Trust's good work! For information, see anglingtrust.net.

Introduction

Unless you live in the small area in East Wiltshire between the villages of Upavon and Netheravon (about ten miles from Stonehenge), you're unlikely to know Martin Aris, and what a shame that is! Martin, aged 70-something but going on 20, works as a river keeper at an old water mill in the little hamlet of Coombe and has many a tale — good, bad and ugly — to tell about country life.

I met Martin when my partner Simon and I were hoping to buy Coombe Mill[1] ('The Mill') in 2015. I tried my best to charm Martin into putting in a good word for us with the then owner, but actually it was Martin himself, and this marvelous place, that charmed us! We were delighted to be successful, and we quickly realised how lucky we were to have such a brilliant bloke on board. Martin does a fantastic job of looking after this thin green strip of land by the River Avon, caring for the marvelous chalk stream river[2] and welcoming the fishermen that come here between April and October each year.

Over the years, Martin has told us many stories about his life in the countryside — first in the Cotswolds (where he grew up) and then in Wiltshire. Many of these tales have made us laugh out loud: they can be hilarious, sometimes shocking, and they often end in his catchphrase: "Unbelievable!"

One day, as Martin was entertaining me with another amusing anecdote, it occurred to me that his life story might make a good book, so I asked him if I could 'interview' him, and he agreed. We started during the early Covid period, over socially-distanced tea breaks, while I was 'working from mill' and Martin was 'working from river'. It seemed appropriate to be embarking on a project like this during the pandemic, when so many of us were reflecting on life and the benefits of getting out into nature.

---

[1] Coombe Mill is just next door to the 'beat' of world-famous fisherman, river keeper and writer Frank Sawyer (1906—1980). Fishing isn't my thing, but Martin says that Frank was one of the greats! A 'beat', by the way, is a stretch of river where the owner of the adjacent land owns the fishing rights.

[2] Chalk streams are rivers that arise through springs from chalk bedrock and flow through chalk land, like we have here in Wiltshire. They tend to have very pure ('gin-clear') water, which is certainly the case here too. Chalk streams are important habitats for wildlife and are sometimes called 'England's rainforests': they're rare and need protecting.

We were both busy, so it took several years in the end, but here we are, better late than never.

Unbelievable! is not like most countryside books today, which tend to focus on nature, posh people or both (e.g. *The Life Cycle of the Lapwing*, or *Lavinia Leaves London to Set up a Llama Farm in Lincolnshire*[3]). Now, there's nothing wrong with books like that, and I have several of them on my bookshelf. This one's just different, for a few reasons, but no less worthwhile reading. Firstly, Martin is a proud working-class man who left school aged 14. Secondly, I've written him up phonetically, in his Cots-Wilts accent, and thirdly, although his story does feature wildlife, it also depicts 'the wild life'. Beware, reader: here you'll find poaching[4], pub fights and saucy bits, embellished with expletives and "Unbelievable!"s.

That said, it's not all fun and games: there's a streak of sadness and nostalgia that runs through the book. Martin describes himself as being 'one of the old breed': a now-rare country bloke who remembers when horses still ploughed the fields. He tells of his regret that 'the old days' are being forgotten, of the changes that he's noticed in nature, and of his worries for the future. There's fear and anger too, in his memories of growing up with a rather violent dad — the thought of whom can bring tears to this otherwise tough guy's eyes.

The book is a hybrid: an illustrated biography in Martin's own words, interspersed with his thoughts on life and nature.

––––––––

[3] Not real books — but they could be! No offence meant to the fictional Lavinia, or to the lapwings.

[4] A slightly serious bit: poaching is part of Martin's life story — it even got him his job at The Mill (read on to find out more). However, poaching is illegal, and Martin's involvement in it was long ago. There's no intent in this book to encourage poaching, or other questionable activities that feature, from nicking apples to punching people's lights out!

It includes musings on the seasons, around which his life and work have always revolved, and which make up the four parts of the book. These are:

Spring — for Martin as a cheeky little boy;

Summer — for his escapades as a young farmer;

Autumn — for middle age, river keeping and family; and

Winter — for later life, with more river keeping and wise words.

The text is a monologue (of Martin's words) but based on many conversations we've had. I've largely relegated myself to the footnotes, but with some thoughts of my own. You might find the footnotes interesting and even amusing, so please take a look!

You might also notice some contradictions in the text: Martin can express strong views on a subject but also happily take the opposite view (e.g. he believes that the old ways are the best, but also that we should go with progress). I think this is great: he's someone who can appreciate the best of both worlds.

I should mention that some names have been changed, for privacy, and that not all of Martin's memories may be 100% accurate. Whose are? I often can't remember what I did at the weekend, let alone what happened decades ago!

Before I start, a couple of additional notes that might help to explain things.

River keeping (and other talents)

You may not know what a river keeper does, and I wouldn't be surprised: it's not a standard career option! So, in a nutshell, the job of a river keeper is to manage and maintain fisheries. It's a practical job, involving tasks such as:

- cutting weeds that grow in the river;
- looking after river banks;
- managing trees;
- sometimes stocking the river with fish (though not in our case — ours is a wild fishery);
- providing security (e.g. from poachers); and
- carrying out conservation projects.

Martin also does lots of mowing, given all the lush grass that grows here by the river. I'd say he's never happier at work than when he's sitting on his trusty ride-on mower, trundling up and down.

However, this river keeper is multi-talented and will turn his hand to anything. For example, when we moved to The Mill we noticed a huge, hollow tree trunk, and I joked that we could make it into a fairy house someday, to entertain little visitors. Martin is a tough, no-nonsense character, so I was very pleasantly surprised when he launched into this not-so-grand design with gusto, just a few days later. Priorities — right? He even bought some plastic fairies to decorate it! Our friends' children loved it, and it was a sign of good things to come.

Martin's English

Please note, I wrote this note before Queen Elizabeth died. I decided not to take her out. Rest in peace, Your Majesty!

And finally, the language. It's impossible to 'hear' Martin in a book, and he'd not like to do an audiobook. However, this is his story, and his accent is an important part of him. That's why I've written it phonetically — as he speaks. It just wouldn't be right to use the Queen's English (aka Received Pronunciation) for Martin: in fact, it would be unbelievable!

When I think of the Queen's English, I think of Queen Elizabeth in her younger years, greeting people with a polite: "How do you do?" — pronounced: "Hauw dooo yooou dooo?" This is an old-fashioned greeting, but Martin's 'old school', and were he to use it, it might sound more like: "Ow ja do?", and I'd write it: "'Ow d' y' do?" This isn't *bad* English; it's just a particular *variety* of English. And, if you tune your ear into how people pronounce their words these days, you'll notice that not even the Queen speaks (spoke!) exactly as it's written. Try pronouncing every vowel and consonant in this sentence, for instance: it's a mouthful!

Now, some people consider the Queen's English to be 'refined', but it's actually much more difficult to write in an accent that's *not* the Queen's English. You also have to consider that a speaker might not pronounce the same word the same way, every time. Martin, for example, uses a mixture of "can't" (A for apple), "cahn't" and "caan't" — with or without the Ts. As well as Martin's accent, I've attempted to capture his manner of speaking: the words he emphasises, the phrases he repeats, and other things an editor might normally take out. All this was a time-consuming task but, as a linguist by background, it was one that I really enjoyed.

To help you with the language — and especially if *English* English isn't your first language — I've added footnotes for any words that might be tricky. These are indicated by a 'T' for Translation. For instance, when Martin says he was born under a goozb'ry bush the footnote is: "T: *gooseberry*". As it happens, I like Martin's way better. After all, he's not talking about geese (goose berries).

The trick is to go slowly: slip into country time and into Martin's riverside world. Think of a 70-something-year-old bloke, relaxing by the river with a cup of tea after a hard day's work, looking up and marvelling at the swallows soaring in the sky. Here goes!

Part One:
Spring

Country lad

I love the countryside — <u>always</u> 'ave done. Well, I w's born 'n' bred out in the country, see? You don' wan' a lot in life when you've got the country like this.

A lot 'f people buy country books these days. Cuz there's more t' life than watchin' the telly 'n' goin' t' the pub...well, goin' t' the pub, that's diff'r'nt![5]

---

[5] Martin loves his beer, and he's spoilt for choice round here, with several great pubs in the surrounding villages. These include The Swan in Enford, The Red Lion in East Chisenbury, and The Dog & Gun and Stonehenge Ales brewery in Netheravon.

International relations

My dad w's German, an' my mum comes from Manchester. She w's in the Land Army in the war — she worked on the farms — an' me dad w's a paratrooper. 'E w's a prisoner 'f war at Lark'ill, well at Rollst'n' Crossroads[6] actually — tha' w's the camp there. They put 'im t' work on the farms, 'n' e got posted up t' the Cotswolds. That's how 'e come to meet me mum[7].

He'd been caught a couple a times, by the Americans, an' 'e got caught twice ov'r 'ere. Sec'n' time, he di'n'[8] wanna go back[9].

'E'd never talk about the war, but 'e <u>did</u> say to us, tha' w's the firs' time 'e'd <u>ever</u> tasted a banana[10]. Yeah, that w's the firs' time.

---

[6] Larkhill, and Rollestone Camp — located near Stonehenge in Wiltshire. The camp housed prisoners of war in World War II.

[7] Some German prisoners of war were permitted to visit British homes and became friendly with local people. Many went to work on farms or in construction. After the war, like Martin's dad, many decided to stay in Britain.

[8] T: *The second time, he didn't want to go back.*

[9] It seems unlikely that Martin's dad was caught and escaped or was set free four times. He may have misremembered or been exaggerating.

[10] This may in fact have been Martin's dad's memory from *after* the war: bananas were not available until then.

Bush baby

I come from the Cotswolds — <u>God's</u> country — Chipping Cam'den[11]. We lived it[12] a place called Longl'n's House[13], an' there w's a farm there. That w's between Chipping Cam'den 'n' Hidcot'[14]. Well, tha' w's a li'l village up there, righ' out in the sticks. 'N' I w's born, nine'-een fifty one, under a goozb'ry bush[15]!

---

[11] T: *Chipping Campden* — a market town in the north of the Cotswolds.

[12] T: When Martin says "*it*" here (and in many other places in the book), this can be translated as "at".

[13] T: *Longlands House.*

[14] T: *Hidcote.* In fact this was two villages — Hidcote Bartrim and Hidcote Boyce — located to northeast of Chipping Campden.

[15] T: *gooseberry.* Being born under a gooseberry bush was a myth told to children, a bit like the stork delivering babies. However, it was actually a euphemism for something rude, which I won't repeat here. Google it if you must!

Sleepy siblings

My firs' mem'ry is sleepin' in a draw at the bo'-m a the old chest 'f draw's.[16] Times w's <u>hard</u> — we di'n' have a lot. Tha's why you appreciate wha' you go' now. A lot 'f people don'.

Well, I w's in the bo'-m draw, an' then, me sister Suzanne w's in the middle, 'n' me brother Lesley (he w's older) w's it th' top. Be-cuz the chest 'f draw's got big, 'n' then star'-ed[17] goin' smaller 'n' smaller. My dad made tha' chest, yeah[18]. I remember tha', cuz we never 'ad a bed!

But, as we got older they <u>'ad</u> t' get a bed, 'n' it w's a bluddy old iron thing — oh! Me sister used t' sleep on the big landin'; me 'n' me brother used t' be in the same bedroom. 'E used t' blame me for f'r <u>ev'rythink</u>. He'd wee the bed 'n' tell me dad it w's me, so 'e wouldn' get a good 'idin'[19]. Yeah!

---

[16] T: *sleeping in a drawer at the bottom of the old chest of drawers.*

[17] T: *started.*

[18] This seems to be the opposite of most chests of drawers, which have the bigger drawers at the bottom and the smaller drawers at the top. However, this one was home made, so it could well have been different.

[19] T: *a good hiding* (beating).

Spring is sprung

You know it's Spring when you wake up. Spring is always where the lambs 'n' the hares are abou', 'n' nature's <u>just</u> star'-in' t' be awake fr'm the winter. <u>Ev'rythink's</u> star'-in' t' come out: bluebells; stuff like tha'.

I like the bluebells, an' I like the snowdrops 'n' the cowslips. I've <u>always</u> liked cowslips. They come out in the Spring.

An' I'll tell you wha' I <u>'aven't</u> seen no more: tha's wild primroses, growin' out in the wild. You don' see 'm no more. I don' know why. You c'd go across the field, when I w's a youngster, and you'd see 'm, 'n' so you'd pick 'm. Same with the vylets[20] — the mauve 'n' the white vylets. I used t' pick a li'l bunch a the mauve ones 'n' white ones f' me mum. But you don' see 'm no more. 'N' I think a lot 'f it is these sprays wha' the farmers use, the chemicals, 'as killed it. I'm <u>convinced</u> 'f it.

---

[20] T: *violets.*

The dawn chorus

T he blackbird is the first bird wha' sings, it four a'clock in the morning; then the rest 'f 'm. 'N' then <u>all</u> 'f a sudden you got the <u>whole</u> choir going! You listen t' that dawn chorus — ah, you couldn' make it up. It's <u>byoodiful</u>![21]

I di'n' realise — it's not until now, when there's not s' much movement, cuz 'f the lockdown[22]... It's so peaceful 'n' quiet now.

---

[21] T: *beautiful.*

[22] Here, Martin was speaking during the first Covid lockdown.

Eggs 'n' apples

We used t' aff t' walk two 'n' 'aa'f miles t' school[23]. Cuz there w's no buses, an' we'd <u>always</u> be late, cuz we'd be birds-nesting — yeah, where you get the eggs out the birds' nests, jus' t' 'ave a collection. It wasn' stealin', nooo, it w's <u>relocatin'</u>! Cuz we'd save 'm 'n' put 'm in sawdust. You cahn' do tha' no more now. You're breaking the law if you do it now.

An' then there used t' be a li'l pond on our way 'ome, an' we'd 'ave the moor-'en[24] eggs, where you'd make a pin prick in 'm. Tha's wha' you did. Y' made a pin 'ole in the top, 'n' a pin 'ole in the bo'-m, 'n' you jus' [slurpppp] blew 'm out! That w's the way 'f doin it so you di'n' break the shell.

Oh yeah, 'n' we used t' go scrumpin' — you know, nickin' apples off people's trees. We'd eat a fair few, til we w's turned green, 'n' ge' belly ache — y' know wha' I mean? The best was, we wen' in this orchard one day, me 'n' my brother 'n' my sister, 'n' there w's some pigs in there. 'N' y' know when you climb the trees, apples'll fall off, won' they, so we kept shakin' 'm off. 'N' then we got bollocked, two days aafter, cuz the pigs w's drunk on apples. Yeah! Tha's why you sh'd <u>never</u> put pigs in an orchard with a load 'f apple trees in there.

---

[23] T: *We used to have to walk two and a half miles to school.*

[24] T: *moorhen.* A moorhen is a black water bird with a red beak, yellow legs and white patches of feathers. We have loads of them here at The Mill!

Udderly delicious

I used t' do the milk it school — the li'l milk bottles in the crate. I'd drink two or three, then say t' the teacher: "They ent given us enough!"

The <u>best</u> w's when you 'ad t' geddit out the cow. That w's <u>old</u> school. You can' beat old school! My dad used t' make us stand in front 'f 'im. 'E'd say to us — cuz I w's the littlest so I went first — 'e'd say: "Open y' mouth!" 'n' 'e'd get the old cow's tit[25] and squirt it, 'n' we 'ad it straigh' from the cow. That w's <u>pure</u> milk.

Ah yeah, 'n' then the cooler, where the milk goes down: we'd 'ave the creeeam off the top, 'n' we'd <u>fight</u> for it. Yeah, that w's <u>brilliant</u> that, I'd f'got about tha'. 'N' then when we 'ad t' churn it fer butter — ah, it took <u>hours</u>! You oughta 'ave a go at that — get some proper milk, put it in a bottle an' shake it, 'n' make yer own butter. Ah it's <u>byoo'-iful</u>[26] — you just add yer salt to it. Yeah.

---

[25] T: *teat.*

[26] T: *beautiful* (this time without a consonant in the middle).

Creepy Crawlies

There used t' be Swan Vesta[27] li'l match boxes, see, 'n' I used t' put earwigs in 'm! An' snails 'n' slugs, 'n' stuff like tha'. I'd catch 'm on the way t' school. Cuz we'd be birds-nestin' on the way, so we w's always late f' school; <u>always</u>.

I used t' 'ave a girl in fron' a me. Dawn w's 'er name, 'n' she 'ad pony tails. She w's nervous all the time — I caan' think why! — so she'd play with 'er 'air <u>auwllll</u> the time, 'n' it w's annoyin' me one day. So I pulled me desk up, 'n' got a box with an earwig in it, 'n' I put it in 'er 'air. 'N' she <u>screamed</u>, be-cuz it come over 'er hair. An' the teacher knew oo it w's, <u>straigh'</u> away. Well, be-cuz if you opened my desk, you'd see I'd 'ave <u>ev'rything</u> in there. I did! I used t' 'ave an old cattypolt[28] in there, marbles; you name it, it w's in there.

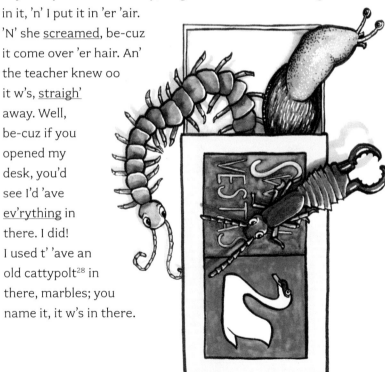

The great escape

One afternoon — I don' know if I w's six, seven — me gran-mum, wha' come down from Manchester (cuz me mum w's born 'n' bred in Manchester), she said summin' t' me 'n' I disappeared. This is wha' they tell me. 'N' next minute, I come down the stairs with me suitcase, 'n' me mum said: "Where you goin'?" I said: "I'm leavin' 'ome." She said: "You got any clothes?" I said: "No, I got me teddy bear in there." Li'l brown suitcase — I'll always re-member it.

'N' I walked up the road t' the li'l triangle, up the top, 'n' I sat there, 'n' I got 'ungry, so I went back 'ome. My gran'ma never ever forgot that. Cuz my mum said: "'E a be back[29]."

But jus' t' take me teddy, ha ha! Not take any clothes or nuffink! Jus' me teddy!

---

[29] T: *He'll be back.*

fun at the fair

When the fair used t' come, when we w's li'l, y'r mum used t' dress you up as diff'r'nt things — cuz it used t' be a <u>faancy</u> dress place before the old fair opened — 'n' she dressed me up as a bumble bee, 'n' I won first prize. I'll always remember tha'. Yeah, they w's good days on that old fair, aw!

But it w's the old-<u>fashioned</u> fair — tha' w's the thing. There w's old bumpers 'n' go round on the merry go round, stuff like tha'. There w's nuthin' like this rubber 'n' elastic where they fly up 'n' all this! Yeah, I loved it, but it's gawn[30].

---

[30] T: *gone.*

Child labour

When I w's eight, I used t' go 'n' work f' the Kite brothers, just up the road from us. 'N' I used t' go in there on a Sat'd'y mornin' 'n' a Sund'y mornin', 'n' I used t' collect all the eggs. I used t' get 'aaf a crown[31], f' tha'.

You'd go in the big old larder — a big room — <u>cold</u> — 'n' you'd aff t' do the butter, <u>all</u> the time, where you just add the salt. I used t' bring that 'ome, 'n' I used t' aff t' give me mum a shillin', save a shillin', 'n' 'ave sixpence t' spend. 'N' that w's a <u>lot</u> a money then, sixpence.

I <u>always</u> remember, we'd go t' Chipping Cam'den with me mum, 'n' she'd 'ave Wolf, our dog, 'n' she'd take the pram t' put the shoppin' in. Be-cuz if you f'got somethin', well, it w's two 'n' 'aaf miles to the shop. 'N' we used t' go t' wh' they called the Black Kettle Shop — big old kettle used t' be above it[32]. We used t' go in there 'n' be <u>fascinay'-ed</u>, looking it all them sweet jars on the counter, 'n' I used t' buy a bag a broken biscuits f'r a hayp'ny[33]. I'll <u>always</u> remember that. 'N' old Wolf, 'e'd sit out by that pram 'n' 'e wouldn' let <u>no</u> one get near that!

---

[31] Half a crown was a coin worth 1/8 of a pound, two shillings and six pence, or 30 old pence. It was discontinued when decimalisation took place in 1971.

[32] The Black Kettle Shop is still there. These day's it's a holiday cottage, but the kettle remains on display, on the front wall.

[33] T: *a ha'penny* (half penny).

four-legged friends

I always 'ad dogs, ever since I w's born, we 'ad dogs. Dogs 'as <u>always</u> been in my life[34]. 'N' Wolf used t' come wi' me, 'n' we used t' 'ave five fields be-ind the cottage, 'n' we used t' walk those five fields, me 'n' the dog, <u>all</u> day. Me mum'd give us a jam samwidge[35], 'n' we'd be gone f' the day, with a bottle a pop, 'n' that'd be it. 'N' we just <u>did</u> things, 'n' sat down, 'n' I used t' talk t' the dog. I don' think 'e ever understood me, but he <u>did</u> when I gave 'im a bit a the jam samwidge! They're better 'n humans. They really are, dogs, they're <u>so</u> intelligent.

'E w's a collie, see Wolf; long-'aired, black 'n' white — 'e w's a <u>beaut</u>! He worked with cows. In the mornin', me dad used t' get up it five, and 'e'd say to us kids: "Right, I'm g'n 'ave cup a tea[36]; take the dog." You'd stand by the gate, open the gate up, 'n' you'd let Wolf go. 'N' d' y' know wha'?, 'e'd go <u>all</u> the way across them five fields. 'N' you c'd count <u>evr'y</u> one a them cows tha' 'e brought back. 'E never ever missed one, tha' dog. 'N' if there w's a cow calvin', he'd go out in that field 'n' 'e'd sit there 'n' 'e'd bark, so me dad w'd know that a cow w's calvin'.

That dog w'd know if there w's a cow missin' be-fore <u>we</u> would. Tha's 'ow intelligent they are. But, 'e 'ad an <u>evil</u> li'l streak in 'im. 'E used t' nip the back a the cows, di'n' 'e, as they w's goin' along. Yeah!

---

[34] Martin got a bit emotional saying this. He really does love dogs!

[35] T: *sandwich.*

[36] T: *I'm going to have a cup of tea.*

Horsing about

Me 'n' my brother, we used t' be sa' on a car' 'orse[37]. One day, me sister w's on the top, 'n' me brother w's underneath the 'orse, cuz 'e w's a dopey old 'orse, 'n' I 'ad goose feather in me 'and, di'n' I[38], 'n' I said: "Look under 'ere." 'N' I w's tickling the' 'orse's balls, an' the 'orse pissed all over me brother's 'ead! Ah, I'll never f'get tha' til the day I die — friggin' <u>unbelievable</u>! Ah, we 'ad many a laaf abou' tha'!

---

[37] T: *We used to sit on a cart horse.*

[38] T: *I had a goose feather in my hand, didn't I?*

Punishment by prune

I can re-member, I <u>hated</u> prunes. 'N' they w's there f' breakfast, dinner an' tea time. In the end I '<u>ad</u> t' eat them. But tha's wha' me dad did. 'E would <u>never</u>, ever waste food. You di'n' eat it in the mornin', it be there at dinner time, 'n' you knew it night, you'd <u>hate</u> it, you'd take your time comin' 'ome from school, just be-cuz you di'n' wan' 'm. But in the end my mum said: "It's bedder just t' eat them 'n' get it over with."

Hot Wheels

Me dad used t' 'ave a mo'-a-bike[39] with a side car, 'n' we used t' get in tha'. 'N' I'll <u>always</u> remember, 'e had a Wolseley four, four, four. We used t' go f' picnics, 'n' me 'n' me brother 'n' me sister used t' stand on the running boards as 'e w's driving, 'n' cling on t' the handle. Cuz there w's no cars about — that w's up the lane, 'n' tha' w's it. Ah, it w's brilliant! Yeah, a lot 'f kids used t' do that, if you 'ad a car going along in Chipping Cam'den, they'd hop on it; 'ave a lift. If you ever got caught... oh! But there w's no police around then, 'an we lived two 'n' a 'aaf miles from Chipping Cam'den then, see, so it di'n' matter.

Me dad used t' say t' me: "Wha'-<u>ever</u> you do, don' open the door until the car's star'-ed an' we're goin' down through the gate." 'N' one day I opened the door, an' 'it put a big dent in the door. A big dent in me <u>aass</u> as well![40]

---

[39] T: *motorbike.*

[40] Dent delivered by dad, not door!

Off t' Church

My dad <u>always</u> used t' say, even when we w's li'l: "Ah, I'm off t' church, I'll see y' lay'-er[41]", 'n' we thought nuthin' of it. 'N' it'd go on fer <u>yurz</u> 'n' yurz[42]. He kept sayin': "I'm goin' a church", 'n' I said t' my mum: "Wha' church does 'e go to?" She said: "The bluddy church with a 'andle on it!"[43] Yeah, it w's a sayin'.

So, me dad's sister come over from Germany, Rita, 'n' me dad said: "Ah, I'm off t' church now, I'll see y' lay'-er." Well, Rita never said nuthin' f'r a bit, 'n' then she said t' me mum: "<u>Never</u> knew my brother went t' church." Me mum said: "<u>I'll</u> show you which church it is," so she took 'er down the pub, 'n' 'e w's in the pub, wa'n' 'e[44]? <u>Gawd</u>, did 'e get a pastin' off Rita, oh! Cuz she w's religious. She <u>dragged</u> 'im out!

Me mum <u>always</u> stipula'-ed, time w's time for dinner, 'specially Sund'y dinner. 'N' my mum used t' say t' my dad: "Dinner a be ready at one." Well, 'e wa'n't in, 'n' this went on f' some weeks. Anyway, me mum jus' put it on a plate, took it down the road, to our local it Chipping Cam'den, t' the Red Lion, put it on the bar, said: "<u>There's</u> yer bluddy dinner." She w's a stick-ler f' time, f' meals.

---

[41] T: *later.*

[42] T: *years and years.*

[43] T: *The bloody church with a handle on it.* Here, Martin's mum was referring to a pint glass with a handle (meaning a devotion to beer-drinking and pubs instead of to religion and church).

[44] T: *wasn't he?*

Blessing the Vicar

All these old sayings, you don' <u>hear</u> 'm no more, tha's the trouble. It's like me dad, 'e'd always say: "Ah, I'm just gunna water the 'orse," or "I'm gunna bless the vicar[45]".

'N' if there w's a woman, you'd say: "'Ave you got clean 'ands?" and if she'd say: "Yeah," I'd say: "Take it f'ra walk!"[46] So, if anybuddy aasks you if you've got clean 'ands, say: "Nooo!"

There's another sayin': "'Ungry must be fed: if you don' feed it, it'll wander[47]." I like tha' one.

_____

[45] Both of these sayings mean to have a pee.

[46] This one is too rude to explain. You'll have to use your imagination!

[47] Ditto, and I don't think Martin was talking about food!

The Merry Widow

In the Red Lion, there used t' be a woman come in there, 'n' they used t' call 'er the Merry Widow. 'N' my dad, 'e <u>always</u> used to be over 'er place. She 'ad more blokes coming out 'er back door than anybody[48]. <u>Chrys'</u>[49], tha's why they called 'er the Merry Widow!

I 'ad an older woman pop me cherry when I w's a young lad — seventeen? I tell yer, my dad w's <u>'orrified</u>! She w's, wha', for'-y three, four'-y four? She w's attractive, but she w's only aafter one thing: she w's after young f'ggin' lads, tha's wha' she w's aafter, tha's it. <u>Unbelievable</u>! 'E w's <u>mor'</u>-ified, my dad.

'N' you <u>always</u> used t' know if a wife's 'usb'nd w's out: she'd let y' know when t' go round, cuz she'd always put the OMO[50] box in the window — Old Man Out. Yeah, the washing powder, tha' w's the way. If the husband w's away, the box used t' be in the window! You don' see that no more, see?

---

[48] No pun intended... I don't think!

[49] T: *Christ*.

[50] OMO was a popular washing powder at the time: this might have been one of the reasons why!

Crime 'n' punishment

Me dad used t' 'ave a cherry belt, cor! That w's a leather belt wha' you 'ave on a big baasket when you go up the trees t' pick the cherries. 'N' I'd get that fer being naugh'-y.

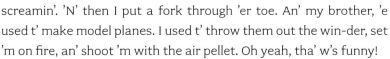

Well, I'd try 'n' put me sister's long 'air in the mangler[51]. 'E couldn't understand why she w's screamin'. 'N' then I put a fork through 'er toe. An' my brother, 'e used t' make model planes. I used t' throw them out the win-der, set 'm on fire, an' shoot 'm with the air pellet. Oh yeah, tha' w's funny!

I used t' aff t' get on me mum's pushbike 'n' go 'n' get the paper f' me dad it six a'clock, so 'e could study 'is 'orses before 'e went t' work. 'N' I went round the bend so faast on my mum's bike, I 'it all the gravel on the side, come off it 'n' bent it. My dad di'n' 'ahf belt me! Ooh, I tell yer — I went 'ome — cor, I couldn' sit down f'r a month! Could not sit down.

But my mum… If we'd done anythink wrong, we'd tell our mum, not me dad. Cuz 'e wouldn' understand; 'e'd 'it us[52]. Y' know wha' I mean? But my mum, she w's always there; always there f'r us. 'N' she w's only five foot nuthin'! She used t' 'ave a hard life, my mum. But she loved gardening, 'n' won a lodda trophies f'r it. Tha's what kept 'er sane f' years.

---

[51] T: *mangle*. A mangle was a machine with two rollers, used to wring out water from wet laundry, before tumble dryers were invented.

[52] T: *he'd hit us.*

The big reckoning

Yeah, my dad w's hard... he w's a <u>haaard</u> man[53]. 'E made my brother go in the Army, but I thought: "Nah, you won't get me, I'm not gunna jump!" Well, I'm not a Yes sir 'n' a no sir, y' know wha' I mean? 'N' I never 'ave been.

---

[53] Saying this brought a tear to Martin's eye.

'E used t' be on the booze... most fathers was in those days, cuz there w's no telly or nuthin'. He came 'ome one night with a couple 'f 'is mates, 'n' 'e got me mum 'n' me sister out 'f bed t' cook food, see, 'n' I said to 'im: "When I'm older," I said: "I'm gunna give you the <u>biggest</u> hidin' 'f your life, 'n' then I'm goin'."

Thing is, '<u>e</u> thought 'e w's doin' the right thing with us but, y' know, you c'n go so far... Well, I wen' the other way. I retalia'-ed against him one day — sorted 'im out. I'm not proud 'f it, but summing 'ad t' be done.

'Ow it 'appened is, 'e came 'ome from the pub, 'n' 'e 'ad a go at me mum. Tha's how it star'-ed. 'N' I said: "I've 'ad enough a this." 'N' 'is attitude w's: "Well, wha' you gunna do abou' it?" But 'e wouldn' fight me with 'is fist, first 'f all. 'E pulled me 'air. 'N' me mum said: "Don't pull 'is 'air!" 'N' 'e did, 'n' 'e tried t' drag me down some stairs. Well, it di'n' 'appen, cuz I '<u>it</u> 'im. Oh yeah! I sat 'im on 'is <u>aass</u>!

I regre'-ed it aafter, but I thought, no — 'e w's bad t' me mum 'n' me sister fer <u>yurz</u>.

'E blamed it on when 'e w's a child, be-cuz 'e 'ad t' join 'itler's Youth[54]. <u>No</u>! Just be-cuz you've 'ad a bad life, don' meant t' say you've godda[55] make your kids 'ave a bad life, 'n' be brough' up like tha'. Tha's why I've <u>always</u> said t' Kyle 'n' Steph'nie[56]: "I'm never gunna treat you 'ow I got trea'-ed, bringin' you up."

I never spoke t' me dad for <u>yurz</u> 'n' yurz aafter tha'. It w's only when 'e had cancer, y' know wha' I mean?

---

[54] T: *The Hitler Youth* — the Nazi organisation for 14—18-year-old male youth.

[55] T: *got to.*

[56] Two of Martin's children.

No pain, no gain

I t w's <u>much</u> harder in our time, but a good 'idin' din' 'urt yer. Y' know wha' I mean? It put you in good stead when you got older — oh yeah, it puts you righ' f' life! I don't stand no nonsense. But I think it w's the upbringing, where 'e w's <u>so</u> <u>hard</u>. 'N' tha's wha's missing t'day, be-cuz if you 'aven't got discipline in the 'ouse you're not g'n' 'ave it outside[57].

We used t' ge' in t' trouble, but we used t' do <u>stupid</u> things — like, when Sergeant Gay used t' come along 'n' go in the pub it night, 'n' we used t' nick 'is pushbike[58] and put it in the apple tree. We watched him one night, go in there, an' we thought 'e'd gawn in the bar — 'e <u>'adn't</u> — 'e'd gawn in and gawn out the back door, 'n' come back round. He <u>knew</u> wha' w's 'appenin', 'n' 'e caugh' us, 'n' 'e said: "Eether I clip your ears or I tell your dad." I said: "You better clip my ears," I said: "It won't 'urt so 'ard!"

---

[57] T: *If you haven't got discipline in the house you're not going to have it outside.*

[58] Pushbike is another term for a bicycle.

Part Two:
Summer

Jump start

I moved t' Wiltsh're when I w's a teenager / twenny one? My dad, 'e said: "Righ', there's a big world out there — go 'n' make it!" Never looked back! I'd <u>always</u> wanned a work on a farm, see, an' my dad wouldn' let me. I would <u>never</u> do wha' 'e told me t' do. Nothin's changed!

When I first came down 'ere, I worked f' Lord 'n' Lady Russell, over it Wylie[59]. It w's all diff'r'nt sorts 'f things — mostly tracter work. Yeah, we did <u>ev'rything</u>.

Tha's when they w's doing the events f' the British Horse Show, with Mark Phillips, so tha's goin' back a bit! He w's one 'f the riders f' the British, wa'n' ee[60]? F' the Gold Cup. Well, the medals, wa'n' it?

Well, Lady Russell, she w's a force t' be reckoned with. She made us put up all the jumps. They went f' <u>miles</u>. Cuz old Lord Russell, 'e'd say to us in the morning: "You all 'ide, she's comin'!" — otherwise 'e'd never get no work ou' 'f us. She'd be in one a them li'l Mini Mokes[61], 'n' if she c'd grab all the blokes she could first thing in the mornin', she'd 'ave us f'r all day. First day I w's there, I 'ad to go on the jumps. She ruled the roost there!

---

[59] T: *Wylye*. The Wylye Valley is in West Wiltshire, between Salisbury and Warminster.

[60] T: *wasn't he?*

[61] A Mini Moke is a small, light car made from the same parts as a Mini.

36

Old Crooky

Then I worked f' Stuart Crook — 'e 'ad the old farm it Coombe[62], wha's not there no more. He owned <u>all</u> these 'ouses down 'ere, the lot. I w's milkin', I w's doin' <u>everythin'</u>.

Cuz I used t' bring the cows down along 'ere, t' The Mill, in the Spring. We used t' flood these fields up 'ere in the Winter, so in the Spring, when the cows w's gonna calve, they'd calve bedder[63], where there's water an' there w's plen'-y 'f graass f'r 'm.

Old Crooky — the bugger nearly caught me twice, poachin' on the big pond. 'E <u>knew</u>. It di'n't matter 'ow craafty you'd think you w's gunna be — tha' man <u>knew</u>. Well, it's godda be experience, to know I w's there.

---

[62] Coombe is the Wiltshire village where The Mill is located, where Martin now works.

[63] T: *better.*

For Pete
(and the other Pete)'s sake

I used t' poach the fish, the deer (go out on the downs), the rabbits. Wha' we used t' do: there w's me, Pete Walker 'n' Pete George: we used t' put the net out — a long net — f' these rabbits. 'N' we'd do tha' quite early, then we'd go down the pub, 'n' 'ave a load a booze, 'n' come out. 'N' you c'd <u>guarantee</u> tha' Pete George would trip over the bluddy nets, an' they'd all ged out.

We nearly shot 'im one day, the other Pete. We w's on a bank, 'n' we said t' this other Pete: "Wha'-ever you do, <u>don'</u> walk in fron' 'f 'm." So if the rabbit come ou' a tha' 'ole tha' side, or this 'ole this side[64], there w's somebuddy there t' shoot 'm. 'N' wha' 'appens? He f'ggin' walks across, dunnee?! God, <u>shit</u>!

---

[64] T: *So, if the rabbit came out of that hole on that side, or this hole on this side.*

Fun with Ferrets

We used t' ave ferrets. I used t' ave some it 'ome. 'N' they're good fer rabbittin', be-cuz you c'n <u>hear</u> 'm — if you put your ear t' the ground, you can 'ear 'm runnin'. But sometimes you'll get a bad ferret, wha' don' wanna come out. 'E's eatin' the rabbit! So you godda dig down 'n' get 'im out.

Old Pete George brought a ferret in the pub one day. Nobody knew, but 'e 'ad it in 'is jacket. Ev'ry now 'n' then you'd see this 'ead poppin' out — it w's <u>'ilaaarious</u>! 'N' I said to 'im: "You ever put tha' down yer trousers, Pete?" "Nooo!" 'e said. I said: "I'll do it, f'r a bet." Wha' you aff t' do, you aff t' tie the bottom a yer trousers with string so it' caan' get out, 'n' tha's wha' I did[65]. 'N' 'e w's <u>'appy</u> as a sand boy[66] down there. 'E di'n't bite me, nooo!

They used t' 'ave ferret races on the fayt[67]. You don' see it no more. There used t' be a ferret woman, wha' lived round one a the farms. She 'ad ferrets. She 'ad <u>hundreds</u> 'f ferrets! She bred 'm 'n' then sold 'm. But people, they don' keep 'm no more.

It's like, did you ever 'ave a little rabbit or anythink when you w's li'l? You 'ad a 'amster. But I <u>bet</u> you di'n't look after it very well. No, see? 'N' this is wha' people do.

---

[65] Reader, please don't try this at home!

[66] Sand boys were boys who used to sell sand in the streets in centuries past. It's thought that they were happy because they were either paid in alcohol, or spent their earnings on it.

[67] T: *fête*.

Poles 'n' pipes

There used t' be a telegraaph pole across the river, to get across fr'm one side to the other, when we come out a the pub. 'N' it's alright if you're sober, but when you're pissed... nooo! 'N' we'd fall in more times than we'd walk across. We used to go down in the pub first,

'n' then we'd go across it. 'N' 'aa'f the time we'd fall in. I don' know wha' ever 'appened t' tha' pole.

Yeah, 'n' there w's a drain pipe too, w' Corine, you know, oo lives down near the church in Fittleton[68]? I knew 'er mum — she used t' babysit f' Stuart Crook, 'n' I used t' see Corine then. So I know 'er ever since she w's li'l. Well, I take the mickey out 'f 'er when 'er 'usb'nd's out — Bob. An' I say to 'er: "Let me know when 'e i'n't there," I say: "leave y' window open 'n' I'll shin up the drain pipe!" Now, if you look at their 'ouse, they 'aven't got a drainpipe, cuz it's thatched roof on there. An' we <u>laaaughs</u> about tha'! Tha's a standin' thing with me 'n' 'er. Cuz there's no OMO boxes, see, so I've got me drainpipe! 'N' she says: "Be-fore you die, I wan' tha' piece 'f guttering."

---

[68] Fittleton is a village neighbouring Coombe.

Fire on the Farm

When I w's working f' Stuart Crook, 'e told me one day: "Go up Coombe Lane 'n' spray the field be-'ind the 'ouses." Well, you i'n't s'posed ter when it's windy[69]. 'N' I said to 'im, but 'e said t' me: "Jus' get up there 'n' do it," 'e said, "it a be <u>fine</u>." Well, I killed ev'rybody's gardens up there. It jus' blew, <u>all</u> across. There w's <u>hell</u> to play[70] over it!

Now, say tha's a square field [Martin draws a square on the table with his finger], 'n' y' know, <u>yurz</u> ago they used t' burn the straw in the field, di'n' they — right? Well, bluddy Stuart Crook said t' me, 'e said: "Get the old tracter," 'e said, "put a tyre on the back," 'e said, "'n' I'll set fire to it," see? 'E said: "Wha' I want you t' do," 'e said: "I want you t' go round the outside 'f the field 'n' work yer way in," — see, not thinkin' — so tha's wha' I did. I <u>never</u> ever lived tha' down.

---

[69] T: *Well, you aren't supposed to when it's windy.*

[70] T: *hell to pay.*

Summer 'n' Cider

I like summer —
it's nice 'n' 'ot.
Cuz when I worked
on the farm I used
t' like doin' the
combining. I loved
tha' job — y' know
wha' I mean?

When we w'z
li'l, the old farmer's
wife used t' come
out with the picnic,
'n' the old farmer'd
give us a drop a
cider. Well, you don'
get the picnics no
more, out in the field. Them days are gone, 'n' it is a shame. It's so
advaanced now, the summer. It's not the same no more. One man
t' do ev'rythink, cuz the machinery's so big.

I like the old ways, with the old Suffolk punch[71], 'n' the old
'orses where they were ploughin'. There's still one man ploughs,
in Hampshire, 'n' 'e wins ev'ry match — an' his son 'as got all the
modern equipment, an' 'e still does ev'rythink with a horse. So if 'e
breaks down 'is 'orse don' break down, see?

---

[71] A Suffolk Punch is not a type of alcoholic beverage (as I first thought when Martin
said this) but a large, chestnut-coloured breed of horse, used for doing heavy work
like ploughing. Also known as a Suffolk Horse or Suffolk Sorrel.

Soaring swallows

The old swallows are about again, now. They've come back in. Tha' means summer's comin'. These swallows, they know when t' come back 'ere, don' they? How they know, I <u>do</u> not know. In the old days, tha's the way you c'd tell wha' month it wuz, when the swallows turned up, an' when they went. They'd go September—October time. So you di'n' need a calender. Diff'r'nt birds, diff'r'nt months. You think about it: it's not rocket science.

But jus' look at 'm, flyin' about 'ere. The higher they go, tha's 'ow far the insects are. The lower they come — <u>whoosh</u>! — when they come on tha' water[72]. <u>Marvellous</u> to watch 'm dive down there, innit, on tha' water, 'n' back up, just like a jet. Yeah. <u>Brilliant</u>!

---

[72] As he said this, Martin was watching swallows wheeling in the sky above the mill pond and diving down, snapping up insects.

Lovely lapwings

I likes t' see lapwings about too — yeah, lovely! They go divin' about ev'rywhere.

You see 'm out on the downs. Yeah, you'll see there's some squares been ploughed up so they can go on there, cuz they like stony ground, 'n' tha's where they nest. You godda be really good t' spot 'm, an' their nests, be-cuz they look like the ground. 'N' you'll get ph'tographers go out there 'n' take pho'-a-graaphs 'f 'm. 'N' if you get too close to 'm they'll dive bomb on yer; they'll swoop down — oh yeah — try'n' a get you away fr'm the nest.

Great big bustards

An' d' you ever see the Great Bust'd[73] up on the Plain[74]? Tha's a bluddy big bird! The buggers won' fly though — they <u>lazy</u>[75]! The foxes used t' get 'm — well, the l'il 'uns anyway, an' the eggs. But they say one a the big ones c'd '<u>ave</u> a fox, if he wanned to[76]. 'N' there's a Land Rover, goes t' the village hall it Enford[77], an' it' takes people up there t' see 'm. But I've never seen one — the bust'd, not the Land Rover!

---

[73] T: *the Great Bustard*. The Great Bustard is a bird that's similar in shape to a turkey, but larger. It's believed to be the heaviest flying bird on earth, although it doesn't fly often. As a global species, Great Bustards are classified as 'vulnerable'. However, the charity The Great Bustard Group (GBG) operates a Great Bustard programme in Wiltshire, just a Land Rover's drive from The Mill. Until the charity reintroduced them, Great Bustards were fully extinct as resident birds in the UK. Happily, the population is now self-sustaining, but GBG monitors their nesting and works with farmers to either protect nests in place or rescue them. They're definitely worth a Land Rover visit — it's fascinating! See greatbustard.org for info.

[74] Salisbury Plain.

[75] The bustards may not actually be lazy — just very happy where they are, in beautiful Wiltshire!

[76] T: *One of the big ones could have a fox if he wanted to* (i.e. kill the fox).

[77] A village next to Coombe.

Love 'n' marriage

Was I ever married? Oh yeah, <u>Chrys'</u>, I w's married twice! Me first one, Bev, w's down in the white 'ouse, down 'ere it Coombe, when I worked fer um... Stuart Crook. Yeah.

I used t' aff t' bike from Harn'm[78], it four a'clock in the mornin', to do the milkin', an' I 'ad t' do tha' f'r a month to prove I wanned the house. Tha's wha' y' did, if you wanted the job, yeah. Cuz I used t' live with 'er in 'Arn'm[79], with 'er parents, and then I got the house, down 'ere. Tha' w's the ninetiz[80]. Yeah, cuz I 'ad an old Triumph Herald car then — my <u>God</u>!

The first one, Bev, I only wen' with 'er cuz I liked 'er legs. Cuz she 'ad <u>nurse's</u> legs. 'N' I said to 'er: "Cor, you've got a lovely pair a legs!" 'N' she w's sat up it the bar in the pub. She di'n' know wha' t' say. So we got chattin'. But it w's 'er <u>legs</u>!

An' I got two older daugh'-ers with Bev. Oh <u>Chrys'</u>, I don't 'ang about! One's now thirty-odd. The other one — she godda be early thirtiz.

---

[78] T: *Harnham*, close to Salisbury, is about 13 miles away from The Mill.

[79] T: *Harnham* again, just pronounced differently!

[80] T: *the nineties.*

The Stag and Bull

An' the worst thing: it w's my stag night, when I w's getting married t' Bev. Stuart said: "I'll take y' down the Red Lion" — there w's whole load 'f us went — the Red Lion at Chisenb'ry[81]. Tha' w's when old Bernard 'ad it, when they 'ad shove-haypn'y[82] in there, 'n' skittles on a string, 'n' then you 'ad tha' bull ring where you goddit on a rope, 'n' you 'ad ter put it round the post 'n' on t' the hook.

---

[81] T: *East Chisenbury*, a village near to Coombe. The Red Lion (East Chisenbury) is a brilliant local pub that we'd recommend. Martin and his dad both drank in the Red Lion (albeit one in the Cotswolds and the other in Wiltshire). Apparently 'The Red Lion' is the most common pub name in the country!

[82] T: *Shove ha'penny*. Shove ha-penny was a pub game involving coins or discs on a rectangular board, placed on a table top.

Well, 'e doctored my drink, di'n' 'e? An' next morning I 'ad go milkin', see, it five. Well, I got there it six. 'N' I <u>always</u> f'get: when you bring cows in, you bring the bull in, be-cuz 'e likes a bit a cake[83]. 'N' Old Cyril, oo w's the 'ead dairyman there, 'e said: "Wha' are you doin'?" I said: "I caan' get these tits on." He said: "Yer only try'n' a put it on the bull!" I w's pissed as fart, pissed as fart — <u>unbelievable</u>! I tell you, I <u>never</u> lived tha' down!

'N' then me 'n' Hans Po-shay[84], oo lived in the bungalow down there, 'e' worked on the farm: as you come back from Chisenb'ry, you got tha' li'l road wha' goes off to them 'ouses, innit? Well, me 'n' 'im w's pissed as fart. 'N' I 'ad a Triumph 2000 then, 'n' I said to 'im: "I'll drive back, <u>I</u> know where we're goin'." Well, we went into this f'ggin' li'l lake, di'n' we? I tell you wha', we did some <u>daaft</u> things then.

---

[83] When Martin mentioned cake here I imagined a bull tucking in to a big nice slice of Victoria Sponge, which I did think was a bit odd — even unbelievable! Later on, I found out that 'cake' is actually a form of compressed food for cattle, containing lots of protein. Ah, I thought, that makes more sense!

[84] T: *Pocher*. Hans Pocher was a Polish man and prisoner of war with Martin's dad — though it's not clear why Hans, as a Polish man would have been a PoW, given Poland was our ally... Anyway, they worked on farms together, in Wiltshire and Gloucestershire, and then later Martin got to know him too.

'Ere comes trouble

I've been banned from <u>all</u> 'f the pubs round 'ere, over the yurz. Pete[85] it the Swan keeps sayin' 'e's gunna ban me. When I go in there 'e says: "Oh, 'ere comes trouble!" I say: "It's only trouble if somebuddy starts." Cuz I won' put up with it — even now.

Like, not s' long back, when Kevin[86] moved 'ere, he said: "We go down the Swan t'night[87]?" I said: "Yeah". 'N' there w's them young lads workin' be-ind the bar in there. There w's a smart-aass one — wouldn' do nuffin' — well, 'e kept givin' me a load a lip, see?

[85] Pete is the landlord of The Swan at Enford, our brilliant, award-winning local pub. We recommend it highly! theswanenford.co.uk

[86] A neighbour

[87] T: *Shall we go down to the Swan tonight?*

'N' I said: "'Ere," I said: "'ave respec' f' y'r elders." 'N' 'e went <u>on</u> 'n' <u>on</u>. Well, I w's jus' goin' be-ind the bar — I w's gunna put 'im on 'is <u>aass</u>! But Pete's missiz[88] came out, 'n' she got rid 'f 'im. She come over 'n' apologised. I said: "I won' put up with it!" Anybuddy oo lips me, they godda 'ave it! I don' give a shit! Never 'ave done, never will do. But tha's it. See, this is wha' I mean. You got the youngsters, an' they think they're the bee's knees.

’Ave I knocked someone out cold before? Yeah — 'n' I w's drivin' it the time! The bloke w's sat next t' me. It w's up in Chipping Cam'den. His dad owned the buildin' firm, 'n' 'e suppor'-ed Coventry, so 'e w's shit anyway! 'N' 'e kept <u>on</u> 'n' <u>on</u> — y' know 'ow people, they just keep on 'n' on 'n' on? It w's reaction — I di'n' even know I done it: <u>baaang</u>, 'e w's out!

An' I <u>'ave</u> spent some nights in a cell. Yeah, Salzb'ry[89]. I've been in there a few times. Be a load 'f us[90], go out, get pissed, 'n' then I'd go along the f'ggin' shop windows — <u>Bam</u>! <u>Bam</u>! Well, they'd 'ad enough.

I <u>'ave</u> quietened down now. All I want is a peaceful life now. But don' get me wrong, I still won' back down. I don't care oo they are or 'ow big they are, y' know wha' I mean? You got' 'old yer ground[91]: at th' end a the day, tha's wha' life's all abou'.

---

88 Emma, the landlady at The Swan, and a primary school headmistress. A busy woman!

89 T: *Salisbury.*

90 T: *There would be a load of us.*

91 T: *You've got to hold your ground.*

Family man

Ah the best: my brother — it w's their boy's eighteenth birthday, right? 'N' they w's in a pub down in Gravesend, 'n' a bloke star'-ed on 'm[92]. 'E's s'posed t' be 'ard man, in this pub.

Well, I w's in Salzb'ry on the merry merry, on the old piss, and they rung me. 'N' they said: "We got a bit 'f trouble down 'ere." I said: "Where's your dad then?" 'E said: "Well, 'e's it the par'-y, it home. We rung 'im but 'e ain't come round." I said: "'Old on," I said: "I'll be down there".

So I paid a taxi bloke two 'undred quid, take me down there. We got there seven a'clock it night, 'n' I walked in t' the par'-y 'n' the boys were there. I said: "C'mon lets go round the pub — let's 'ave a look 'n' see this bloke." So we wen' in this pub, never said a word to 'im, <u>bang</u>! Tha' w's 'im, <u>finished</u>.

So I went back t' the par'-y 'n' I did the same thing t' my brother. He got up, 'e said: "Wha' you do tha' for?" I said: "Don't aask again." I said: "You look after yer kids."

So they locked me up f' the night; told me never t' come back down t' Kent again.

---

[92] T: *a bloke started on them* (i.e. got aggressive with them).

Bumpy start

Old John Salvage (me next boss), 'e w's a <u>hard</u> man, 'n' 'e 'ad 'ands like shovels, tha' man[93]! An' if you did summink wrong 'n' you w's in a tracter, 'e'd 'ave yer 'ead there, cor, 'e'd knock y' about, 'n' then get rid 'f yer. Tha's the sort a man 'e was.

You used t' get the hunt, used t' go all around Tidworth. Well, they used t' leave some a the gates open. 'N' tha' John Salvage, 'e got the huntsman t' come out on a Mond'y morning, 'n' 'e come

---

[93] T: *He was a hard man, and he had hands like shovels, that man!*

down that yard 'n' got hold 'f 'im like tha' [Martin raises his fists], 'n' lifted 'im up in the air. 'E said: "You <u>ever</u> come 'ere again 'n' I'll <u>shoot</u> the bluddy hounds." 'N' tha' bloke shit 'imself, he <u>really</u> did!

One day 'e said t' me, 'e said: "Let's go round the corner," 'e said, "'n' let's 'ave a fight." I'd come out the workshop 'n' I said: "Come on then!" I 'ad a lump 'ammer[94] in me 'and — tha' would've been the only way you'd beat him. So I said: "You keep comin'; you keep comin'…" An' 'e never did in the end. But my God, 'e 'ad 'ands like shovels!

Another time, 'e let 'is bluddy li'l terrier run round the cattle in the crush[95], annoying 'm when I w's try'n' a put 'm up in the trailer. 'N' 'e said t' me: "Go in there 'n' get the old dog out," so I did, huh. F'ggin' buttin' me ev'rywhere, they was, in there. An' one 'f 'm kicked me in the 'ead, oh!

I still got the dent there now, right it the front. 'E said: "I'll take yer back to the farm," 'e said. 'E said: "D'you want glaass a whiskey?" I said: "Yeah, I'll 'ave glaass a whiskey." I must've had 'aa'f the bottle, I think.

Oh, I 'ad ter go t' th' hospi'-l next day be-cuz there w's a nurse lived in one a the 'ouses, an' she said: "I think you better go ter hospi'-l, jus' ter see if they can see anythink." I said: "Well, I got nuthin' up there anyway so it's a waste a time!" But it w's fine.

Years ago I used t' get <u>reeeal</u> bad 'eadaches, 'n' the doctor used t' give me the biggest painkiller 'e could find. It's not s' bad now, but when I w's younger, my kids, they <u>knew</u>, if I w's quiet, they knew t' stay away from me. Cor yeah, I used t' 'ave <u>vile</u> headaches. Yeah, tha's the dent, jus' there, near my personality box!

---

[94] T: *lump hammer*. A lump hammer is a heavy hammer used for driving stakes or breaking stones.

[95] A crush is a cage for large animals such as cows, to hold them safely while they're examined or treated, or before they're transported.

Town mice, country mouse

My second wife w's Kath. My first missus buggered off with some bugger else. Well, they both did. They thought the graass w's greener on the other side — well, it wasn'!

I makes the wrong mistake ev'ry time: I married someb'dy from the city. It don' work if you're country, it <u>don'</u>! Y' know: if I say: "Le's go f'r a walk," they say: "Wha' d' I wanna go f'r a walk for?" Know wha' I mean? No, tha's where it goes all wrong. If you're gunna get married 'n' you're country, marry a <u>country</u> girl. Cuz they'll 'ave the same things as you.

Yeah, everything in my life happened in ten yurz; ev'ry ten yurz. <u>Weird</u>, tha' wuz! Cuz when I married Bev I w's thir'y two, 'n' when I married Kath I w's for'y two. She already 'ad Steph'nie, but Kyle w's my love child. Well at for'y two...

Love 'n' lorries

Kyle w's born nine-ee-nine, 'n' 'e w's conceived in the back 'f a 'merican lorry. Tha's how 'e come abou'. 'E don't know tha' — 'e will now! Well, I used t' go with a mate 'f mine, Colin, it Tidworth. 'E 'ad all American vehicles, an' I used t' drive one a the ten tonners. So when I met Steph'nie's mum, I took 'er with me. We used t' go away f' weekends with 'm all, where we'd go t' these shows with the vehicles. That's 'ow Kyle come abou'. Yeah, an' it w's absolutely <u>pissin'</u> down with rain.

Steph, she's...wha' is Steph? Twenny eight? Cuz I've 'ad Steph'nie since she w's five, I've 'ad Steph'nie. But Steph'nie come 'n' live with me ten yurz ago, when 'er mother decided she'd f'ck off with another man, t' Preston, and she di'n't wanna go. An' she got rid a Kyle, said: "You c'n 'ave 'im." Cuz I lived on the barge[96] be-fore then, see? I <u>loved</u> it on there. So I 'ad t' come off the barge... well, I di'n' <u>haff</u> to, but when she star'-ed messin' abou', tha's when I come off the barge, took the kids with me an' got the cottage out in the field. Cuz they'd 've 'ad no life up there in Preston — none at all.

---

[96] Martin lived on a barge for several years — see later for details.

Sneakin' about

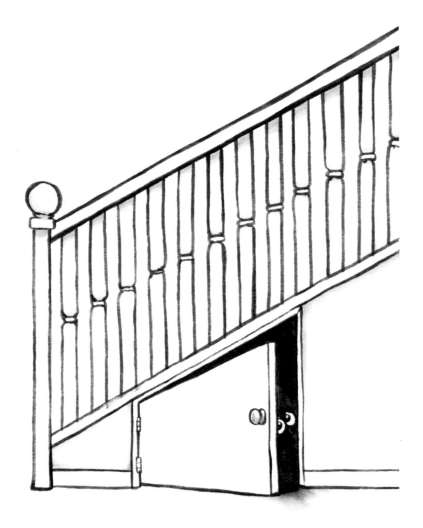

An' then there wuz Rosie. I knew Rosie thirty yurz ago, nah, maybe a bit longer. I used t' go t' Country 'n' Western, an' I met her there. This w's before Bev 'n' Kath came on the scene, yeah.

Well, she w's goin' with this bloke. 'E w's a right...[97]. Yeah, 'n' we star'-ed a go out — sneak out — fr'm the Country 'n' Western. Anyway, this wen' on f' some time. An' anyway, they moved fr'm Andover t' Basingstoke, see? 'N' then they moved back abou' ten yurz aafter. An' she rung me one day 'n' said: "I'm back in Andover." So I said: "Yeah, you still go t' Country 'n' Western?" "Yeah" she said. So we go t' Country 'n' Western, 'n' <u>'e's</u> there, 'n' 'e shakes me by the 'and 'n' says: "Awright mate?" I said: "Yeah, no problem." Well, 'e 'ad "n <u>inklin'</u> but 'e wa'n't sure[98], cuz I w's too craafty.

Then I met Bev, 'n' then we just drifed fer ten yurz, 'n' then when Bev buggered off, Rosie come back on the scene. An' this time, she come 'n' moved in with me over it Tidworth, on the farm. 'N' we w's in the yaard one Frid'y or Sat'd'y mornin'. We w's puttin' a radia'-er in the tracter, 'n' old John Salvage, 'e said t' me: "There's a bloke out 'ere," 'e said, "by the shed, lookin' fer you." I said: "Oh aah?" I said: "Well, send 'im in then." So old John sends 'im in t' me. 'E said: "Awrigh' mate?" I said: "Yeah, no problem!" 'N' 'e put 'is arm round me 'n' said: "D' you reck'n I c'd 'ave me wife back?" I said: "Well, if <u>she</u> wants t' go with yer, tha's fine," so I 'ollered across the yard — I said: "Rosie, you wan' go back wi' 'im?" "Nooo!" she said. Anyway, 'e must've kept ringing 'er: eventu'ly, week or two weeks, she wen' back. But I knew it woudn' work. Cuz she come back again. 'N' then, when she <u>did</u> finally go back, it wuzn' workin'.

I thought, I'll keep ou' a the way f'r a bit. So I did, 'n' tha's when I met Steph's mum, Kath, in the Clarry Club[99], it Tidworth. Cuz I used t' do the bouncin' on the door in there. I never f'get, when we

---

[97] There would have been a juicy swear word here, but Martin's chain of thought moved on too quickly, so I never found out what it was!

[98] T: *he had an inkling but he wasn't sure.*

[99] The Clarendon Sports and Social Club.

start'-ed goin' out I kept pesterin' 'er, 'n' in the end we wen' out. She di'n' tell me she 'ad any kids, but I <u>knew</u> she 'ad kids. 'N' 'er old man[100], 'e's s'posed t' been on exercise ('e w's in the Army). Well, the bugger turned up, di'n' 'e, while I w's round 'er place. So I 'ad t' go underneath the stairs in the cupboard. 'N' Steph'nie seen me go in there, 'n' 'er mum said: "<u>Don'</u> you tell your dad 'e's there." 'N' Steph'nie'll tell yer, she said: "I <u>knew</u> you 'adn't gone, cuz I see you go underneath the stairs."

'N' then we'd go to Andover, 'n' Rosie w's workin' in tha' jewellers where they do yer ear piercin' 'n' all tha'. An' as it 'appens, Kyle said t' me, 'e said: "Can I 'ave me ear pierced?" I said: "Yeah." 'E said: "I'll only 'ave it pierced if you 'ave <u>yours</u> pierced." Well, we walked in there 'n' oo's workin' in there? Rosie! Well, you'd think there w's <u>thunder</u>, with Kath. Oooh, she 'ated her, sheee <u>hated</u> 'er. <u>Unbelievable</u>, it wuz.

Rosie come on the scene again only five yurz ago, but she wa'n't with 'im; she w's on 'er own. I 'elped 'er t' move into a flat 'n' all tha', 'n' we wen' out f'r a bit, but it wa'n't the same. She wa'n't the same Rosie I knew tha' I knew. In the end, she moved away, 'n' tha' w's the end 'f tha'. But yeah, I 'ad some good years with 'er. We 'ad some fun, my <u>God</u> if we di'n' — sneakin' abou' ev'rywhere!

---

[100] Here, Martin meant Kath's husband at the time.

Martin's parents, Pat and Guneter, on their wedding day (1943).

Three smiley siblings: cheeky grins from left
to right: Lesley, Suzanne and Martin.

Not quite so cute but still cheeky: Martin as a teenager at a country fair, meeting a man with a monkey, as you do!

Too cool for school — more monkeying about.

Martin as a young farmer, working out which
one was the bull (only kidding)!

Martin in his bouncing days.

Family man: Martin on the school run with Steph,
country-style. Apparently all Steph's classmates
were jealous that she got to travel by tractor!

River keeping: Martin clearing out weed from the river.

Four friends: Martin, Simba, Cokey and Simon (my partner).

The best day of Martin's life — his son Kyle's wedding.
There were tears and beers.

Autumn days

I love Autumn. 'Specially if you go down the forest[101], down South-ampton, 'n' 'specially on a Sund'y morning.

We used t' camp down there — me, Kath 'n' the kids — 'n' you used t' see the deers. You used t' get up in the mornin', 'n' it looked so byoo'-iful, where you see the deers in the distance, with the old leaves comin' down. Brilliant! Be-cuz the change 'f them leaves is unbelievable! Man couldn' create tha' if he tried.

Yeah, Autumn is the best time a the year. When ev'rythink's on the change, 'n' you know winter's comin'. 'Specially those three trees down the bo'-m 'f the lawn there[102], over by the wood shed. Cuz they change in the Autumn, all diff'r'nt colours. It's fascinating, cuz I think sometimes: "Well how d' they do tha'?" Cuz a tree must 'ave a brain, it must, t' tell it wha' t' do. 'N' if you ged a glaass 'n' put it against a tree, you can hear it drinkin' the water up. I bet you never knew tha'. They're alive!

---

[101] Martin is referring to the New Forest, which covers parts of Hampshire and southeast Wiltshire.

[102] Martin is referring to three trees in the garden at The Mill, whose leaves turn particularly beautiful colours in the Autumn.

A poacher, poached

I've been workin' 'ere at The Mill, oh <u>Chrys'</u>! ... twenny five yurz? Firs' f' John Sharp, 'n' now f' you 'n' Simon.

'Ow it 'appened w's I w's poachin' up the top. Tha' bit 'adn' been fished fer <u>yurz</u>. I got some fish f' the pub, 'n' there w's someb'dy else in the pub an' said t' me: "You w'n' get <u>me</u> a coupla trout, would yer[103]? I got some friends comin' over t'morra." I said: "Yeah, I'll get y' some."

Well, I came back t' the same place. But wha' gets me is, the old boss, I reck'n he knew. Cuz why w'd you be walkin' up there late it night? <u>Tha'</u> w's the problem.

'N' 'e give me the option: 'e said: "Right," 'e said, "y' got two choices 'ere: you c'd 'ave a job 'ere — be a poacher 'n' stop a poacher — or we c'n 'ave a walk t' the magistrates." So I said: "Right, I'll 'ave the job." An' I been 'ere ever since!

'E w's a good boy, John Sharp. A very shrewd man, 'e was. About twenny <u>yurz</u> I worked f'r 'im.

---

[103] T: You wouldn't get me a couple of trout, would you?

Riveting riverkeeping

It ent a job 'ere, it's a holid'y. It's not hard work: I'm 68[104] and I can still mow all day. But a lot 'f people would've walked away. It's a good life f'r anybody tha' wants t' be outdoors.

This is me office. I <u>love</u> it 'ere. Always 'ave done. If you're stressed, you walk up tha' river, 'n' you come back down 'n' you've f'gotten wha' you w's stressed about. Tha's true. Be-cuz the

river's calm, 'n' it soothes yer. It's <u>unbelievable</u>. It <u>reeeally</u> is!

An' there's <u>so</u> much nature you can see. I like the otter, and I do like the kingfisher, cuz 'e's so graceful. I like the mu'tjac[105] as well. I think they're <u>marvellous</u> little things! An' we've never 'ad a problem 'ere with the fox.

People don' understand nature. Alrigh', they read it in a book, but you jus' godda sit 'n' watch. It's a marvel, wha' you see!

---

[104] Martin was 68 at the time he said this (this was when I first started taking his story down). A few years have passed but he's still mowing (happily, I think)!

[105] T: *muntjac* (a small species of deer).

Otters, out and about

But yeah, I've always liked the otter. Cuz the otter is a <u>fighter</u>. He <u>will</u> survive, an otter. But an otter's not greedy. Y' know, people say: "Ah, they take all the fish out the river": they don't. They only take out wha' they wanna eat, 'n' tha's it. 'N' t' go <u>twenny</u> miles a day t' look f'r a bitch... Tha's wha' 'e do![106]

Sometimes if you see 'm in the distance you think it's a seal. It's <u>byoodiful,</u> the gracefulness; 'n' jus' like a dolphin, the way it goes over. They really are lovely creatures. 'Aven't seen 'im f' some time, though, the old otter.

---

[106] Otters have large territories, especially dog (male) otters. They're usually solitary, except when breeding. Dog otters may have more than one love interest along their patch, though they don't help with child care: they're too busy being roving Romeos!

Colourful kingfishers

The kingfisher? Oh, I love 'im — <u>byoodiful</u> bird[107]! But I 'aven't seen 'im since they star'-ed nesting. You couldn' do those colours wha' 'e's got in 'is feathers — you really couldn'. When you think, God created — 'n' by God, 'e <u>did</u> create 'm di'n' 'e? — at the end 'f the day, my God!

D' you know wha', I'd like t' know how they got them colours. If you think abou' it... 'N' how did the robin get 'is red breast? They say it w's an arrow[108]. Well, it w'sn' an arrow — y' know wha' I mean? It <u>fascinates</u> me.

---

[107] Kingfishers are one of the very best bits of living/working/fishing at The Mill. As Martin says, they really are beautiful, with their orange, white and bright turquoise colouring, which contrasts with the muted colours of the Wiltshire countryside. Blink and you might miss them: they fly low over the river, but super fast, like feathered fighter jets. However, their high-pitched squeak of a call can alert you that they're in-coming, so you don't miss out on the air show!

[108] There are many myths about how the robin got his red breast: an arrow is just one!

The rat race

I went t' London once, f'r a bluddy 'oliday — never again! Well, nothing stopped f' <u>twenty</u> <u>four</u> <u>hours</u> <u>a</u> <u>day</u>. An' 'specially when we wen' in the club, 'n' you di'n't aff t' pay until you left. Well, they di'n' tell us tha' when we wen' in there. Oof, no! Ooh, I couldn't 'ack tha'[109]. Well, I w's on the train the next day 'n' back down.

I caan' be doing with a lodda people, you know, like London. I couldn' live in the city. It's a rat race 'f people! I used t' <u>hate</u> goin' there when Sharpy lived 'ere, 'n' I had to drive 'im. Nob'dy 'ad time f' nuthin'. An' tha' Undertube[110], cor! I used t' think to meself, how c'n people live like tha'? But, tha's the situation they're in in London. It's a <u>faast</u> place, 'n' you've got t' be on the ball with it. It's alright to go f'r a day, you know wha' I mean? But, nah, I like it in the country. I don't wan' a lot out 'f life, never 'ave done. 'Ave me beer, 'ave me wimmin, 'n' tha's it![111]

---

[109] T: *I couldn't hack that (i.e. stand it).*

[110] T: *Underground.* I just love how Martin refers to the Underground as the Undertube. I shall be using this term henceforth!

[111] T: Have my beer, have my women, and that's it!

Dream dog

Simba[112], 'e w's <u>so</u> intelligen'. Well, how 'e come about: my sister rung me 'n' said: "Thez a woman it Worrickshur is got some German Shepherds[113] — puppies." 'N' she said: "D' you want one?" 'N' I said: "Well, I'll come up 'n' 'ave a look." Well, I went over there, 'n' Simba w's just a ball — tha's <u>all</u> 'e w's! This w's when I w's married t' Steph'nie's mum. She said: "Yeah, we'll 'ave 'im." She said: "I'll look after 'im." Well, she never did. And so 'e used t' come t' <u>me</u> all the time. Cuz I used t' take 'im out 'n' I used t' sit 'n' stroke 'im.

'N' summink 'appened one day, cuz 'e <u>bit</u> 'er. 'N' she said: "You get rid 'f it!" 'n' I said: "No." Dogs don' bit you f' nuthin'. They don' f'get.

---

[112] Simba was Martin's beloved dog, now dead.

[113] T: *There's a woman in Warwickshire who's got some German Shepherds.* Warwickshire is just to the north of the Cotswolds.

Me 'n' Simba 'ad an understaandin' — we really did. I wouldn' go <u>nowhere</u> if I couldn' take 'im. Tha' w's it. He knew. 'N' tha's why 'e'd never let nobody feed 'im at 'ome — only me. Steph'nie w's sayin', 'e used t' sit downstairs by the front door 'n' 'e wouldn' move until I come 'ome. They 'ad t' feed 'im down there.

'E w's such a character. It's like, when the sprinkler used t' be on the lawn, 'n' 'e'd try 'n' chase tha' water <u>all</u> the time. The way 'e'd lay on 'is back 'n' all tha'. 'N' then 'e'd sit 'n' watch me as I come down the river, 'n' tha's it, 'e'd follow me. When 'e w's in the 'ouse, 'e w's sat by me, by the side 'f my chair there, 'n' 'e <u>would</u> <u>not</u> move. He'd stay there.

When I adopted Cokey[114] — ooh, tha' w's a rival — Cokey thought she w's gonna be the bee's knees. Well, labradors they eat anythin', 'n' she went to eat Simba's food, 'n' tha' w's a no-no, 'n' 'e '<u>ad</u> 'er! 'N' after tha', she watched 'n' learned off Simba. Be-cuz she used t' gulp 'er food down 'n' 'ave nothin'. Now she don' do tha' now. 'N' she learnt fr'm Simba, cuz Simba'd only 'ave a bit and then 'e a leave it, 'n' this is wha' she did in the end. Dogs do learn off other dogs!

There's a thing about dogs; me 'n' dogs've always got on well. I'd never get another dog. Simba w's a one off. You get a one off — like Wolf wuz, with my dad all the time — he w's a one off. Tha's three years this year when Simba died. 'E w's sixteen when 'e died.

---

[114] Cokey was a chocolate Labrador that once belonged to the previous owners of The Mill (the Sharps) but who went to live with Martin. She died in 2021 and is buried under a big tree at The Mill, next to her mum.

Fishin' 'n' Chillin'

I love fishing. Fishing 'n' mo'-a-bikes. Well, Simba w's first, 'n' now 'e's gawn, it's fishing now.

I can sit on tha' bank — I don' care if I di'n' catch <u>nuthin'</u> all day — it's the <u>wildlife</u> wha' go by you. People on barges, people walkin' by don' see it. But when you're sat there 'n' you see tha' kingfisher... 'e a come up, 'n' 'e a park 'imself there [115], somewhere, 'n' 'e a go up 'n' down most 'f the day... It's jus' the peacefulness, the quiet. You relax; you jus' chill. 'N' tha's wha' fishin' is about — it's chillin' out. It's a bonus if you <u>do</u> catch a fish, but it's just t' sit there. Y' know wha' I mean? No worries in the world. I switches me phone off 'n' tha's it!

A lot 'f people say t' me when I go fishin': "What're you doing?" I say: "I'm studyin' the water." You sit 'n' you see which way the wind's blowin' it, an' which way the current's goin', 'n' tha's wha' you godda do. You godda be able to read yer water.

---

[115] T: *he'll come up and he'll park himself there.*

Fishermen's Friend

My advice t' the fishermen wha' comes 'ere is: don't come with all the gear but no idea! It's good when you get someb'dy come 'n' they keep asking you about the river: you know they're int'rested in it. You can spot 'm a <u>mile</u> away. <u>They're</u> the ones wha' catch.

T' me, if people come 'ere t' fish — 'n' they pay a lot 'f money t' come t' fish — they wanna catch fish. 'N' they always say t' me when they come 'ere: "You're the only river keeper wha' takes us right round[116]: usually we jus' got a map." I say: "I can show you the fish; all <u>you</u> godda do is try 'n' catch 'm." 'N' tha's wha' they do. I don' like it if yer payin' a lotta money f' summit 'n' they jus' give you a map — be-cuz you don' know how far you godda go up, where the fish are — you c'd be goin' up 'n' down all day 'n' not catch <u>nuthin'</u>!

Now, I knows this river[117] 'n' I know the carrier[118]. I know where <u>ev'ry</u> hole is. There's certain places where fish'll always hold up — y' know, underneath overhangin' trees 'n' braanches; stuff like tha'. Or if you got berries on a tree, or those tiny li'l blue beetles tha' the old trout like — there's food goin' in, 'n' tha's where they hang, see? Oh yeah. Be-cuz if you're on a lake or summink 'n' you're fishin', 'n' you see a fish over the other side, 'n' there's a bush over there — 'specially with red berries — <u>tha's</u> wha' you put on yer 'ook.

You think about it, in the winter, a lot 'f these fishin' places put pellet in the water t' feed 'm. So ev'ry day those fish wait — they know they're gunna get fed. But, if you've got wild fish, where they gunna get the food from? It's when the berries or the beetles drop off the trees int' the water.

---

[116] Martin welcomes the fishermen, shows them up the river and tells them where the fish might be. Not all river keepers do this, apparently, but we think it's a no-brainer! The fishermen give good feedback on this, and on Martin.

[117] The River Avon.

[118] The carrier is the 'natural' (chalk stream) river; in contrast to the 'leat' — a man-made section which branches off from the carrier and, in the old days, used to feed the mill wheel.

Barge life

I lived on the barge a few yurz. I knew things w'sn't goin' right with 'er at home, so I jus' said t' 'er: "I'm goin'." She said: "To work?" I said: "No, I'm <u>goin'</u> — 'ad enough 'f yer." An' tha's when I got the barge.

I <u>loved</u> it on there. Ooh, I used t' get up to some things on there! We used t' park between Pewsey 'n' Wilcott. We used t' park down by the wood. Nob'dy else doesn' park down there cuz they w's frightened tha' the braanches w's gunna come off the trees. An' old Simba used t' go in tha' wood, where the deer w's on this estate, on the Rothman estate, an' the old bugger, 'e come back, an' 'e'd chased one; well, it go straight in barbed wire di'n' it?

Man's best friend

Simba used t' stay out all night on the barge — 'e wouldn't come in. You di'n' 'ave t' lock y' doors with 'im on there. Yeah, well, 'e saved my life when I 'ad 'art attack[119]. Tha's eeleven  years ago, y' know? <u>Chrys'</u>, where's the years gone?!

I w's here it The Mill it dinner time, takin' a big piece 'f wood out the sluices[120], 'n' I wen' all dizzy 'n' sweaty — tha' w's the start 'f it. So I sat down 'n' I w's fine. I went back t' me barge about ten a'clock it night. I got ready f' bed 'n' got in the bed, 'n' all a sudden I knew I w's 'avin' 'art attack. I <u>knew</u>. 'N' tha's when I dialled 999, 'n' they said: "Where are you?" I said: "I'm on a barge between Wilcott 'n' Pewsey," 'n' they said: "Well, try 'n' get out 'f the barge," so I did: I wen' up the steps, an' that's the laast I remember.

So they said t' me, when they got there, Simba w's laid on top a me, kept me warm, cuz this w's in Feb'ry[121] 'n' I only 'ad t-shirt on, be-cuz the barge is all metal, but 'e wouldn' let the ambulance or air ambulance people get t' me, so they 'ad t' get a p'liceman there. Fair play, they put Simba in the barge 'n' 'e stayed in there all over night.

Next morning, one a the neighbours came over with my ex, Kath, t' pick Simba up, 'n' then 'e used t' bring 'im t' the 'ospital t' visit me.

---

[119] T: *when I had a heart attack* (nothing to do with painting!).

[120] Sluice gates help to manage the river water. At The Mill, they can be lowered to channel water towards the mill wheel (to turn it so it would operate), or they can be raised to direct water into the mill pond and away from the house, for example in case of high water.

[121] T: *February.*

Okey Cokey

I'll never f'get Simba, but yeah, Cokey's a good dog. She waits f' me, see? Soon as I come in it night, don' matter if Steph'nie's jus' took 'er out 'n' across the field, she'll wait fr <u>me</u> to take 'er out. 'N' then, when I've 'ad me tea, I'll sit down, 'n' she'll look at me, 'n' I'll say: "Come on then!" 'N' she'll sit down in front a me, 'n' I aff t' stroke 'er belly. She likes me t' stroke 'er belly with me feet. 'N' then she'll go daaft an' oooh, aaahhh 'n' all this! She's a real loveable dog.

Buzzard bullets

Dinner time Mond'y, I took Cokey out in the field, like I always do, 'n' I w's watchin' this buzzard, 'n' 'e w's in a thermal, 'n' I watched 'n' I watched 'im, 'n' 'e w's goin' up an' up an' up... 'n' then all a sudden, 'is wings went back, 'n' 'e w's like a bluddy bullet, <u>whoosh</u>! <u>Chrrrys'</u>, did 'e ever go! Now I've never, ever seen <u>tha'</u> be-fore. I di'n't realise they c'd go s' faast.

Seasonal slog

Ev'ry month, there is <u>always</u> something you haff t' do, as a river keeper. You godda maintain ev'rythink. It's no good lookin' ad it 'n' think: "Well, I'll do tha' sometime." You godda get on with it! An' you know, if you leave a job 'n' you come back to it lay'-er on, it's <u>hard</u>. It's like, if you miss a week 'f mowin', there's twice as much t' mow, so it's gunna take yer twice as long. So tha' stops you doin' somethin' else.

I make li'l pools in the river, so if the water's low, there's enough water f' the fish. Ev'ry time when the fishermen are 'ere, tha's where the fish hold, in the deep water. You 'ave t' <u>create</u> things in the water. It's like, on the back piece there just before you get up t' sec'n' pond[122], I put a big piece a wood in over the far side 'f the carrier, in the water, 'n' the fish'll go underneath there. See, they like protection. They likes t' <u>hide</u>.

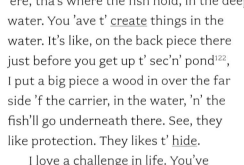

I love a challenge in life. You've godda 'ave sumthin' to aim for in life. I can do most things. I've taught meself on a lot 'f it. It's <u>unbelievable</u> — it really is. 'N' I shall never retire — tha's a sure thing!

---

[122] T: *second pond* (a pond about half way up the river bank).

fighting floods – the no-nonsense way

With river keeping, flooding is yer priority. This is all flood plain fields, see? Be-cuz when I w's on the farm, that's wha' they used t' do, yurz ago. They used t' 'ave the old wooden sluices in the ground. You used t' open those up in the winter, t' flood the ground, so in the Spring you could put cattle out there — the cows what's gunna calve.

When I first came 'ere, we 'ad one flood, an' you c'd see when it w's comin' up. So, where the first dip[123] is, wha' I dug out, I always used t' 'ave tha' as my marker. Be-cuz once tha' water star'-ed comin' up, if you di'n't 'ave tha' f'r it t' go in the river, it'd come down t' the house 'ere. 'N' they'd say, like, awright, if it rains tomorrow, tha' water won' come down this river until the next day. Tha's when you open all the sluices up. It takes twenny four hours f'r it t' come down. When people say: "Cor, tha' were a lodda rain we've 'ad," you wait til the next day. At eleven, twelve a'clock, tha's when it rises. You godda study the water, you godda <u>understand</u> it.

Ah no, you don' want all this concrete 'n' bluddy steel 'n' stuff in there. They never 'ad it yurz ago: it w's all wood, 'n' it worked. See? Tha's the thing. This is why I say the river people[124] make things too <u>complicay'-ed</u>.

———

[123] A small dip in the ground that Martin created to channel water towards the mill pond and away from the house.

[124] The environmental authorities, who visit The Mill from time to time.

Respec' f' yer elders

I have fallen in the river a few times 'ere, yeah, an' chucked a few people in. Like, one a the neighbour's boys — I chucked him in sec'n' pond! Well, 'e kept gobbin' it[125]. I hate youngsters gobbin' it t' me. 'N' I did say t' 'im: "You keep gobbin' it t' me 'n' you're goin' in." Well, 'e w's in. 'Is dad said 'e's never f'got tha'. Well, I won't have younger generation gobbin' t' me. You godda 'ave re-spect. An' tha's what's missing in this day 'n' age, is re-spec' f' yer elders. If you don't try 'n' educate 'm... Well, they're runnin' riot in Brixt'n now, i'n't they?[126]

Ah! Wha's goin' on with this world? This is why I feel sorry for the youngsters t'day — the li'l 'uns, the toddlers, what's comin' on. Wha' life are they goin' 'ave when you got idiots like them rioters, in this world? An' they s'posed t' be educay'-ed people to run this country when us old 'uns are gone. It ain't goin' 'appen. I don't want t' be 'ere in bluddy eigh'-y years' time, Chrys'! Things are gunna change a lot, 'n' it ain' gunna be f' the bedder. Cuz 'aa'f the people wha's in power ain' got a clue wha' they're doin'.

---

[125] 'Gobbing it' means being rude and disrespectful.

[126] At the time of this chat there were riots under way in Brixton.

Part four:
Winter

Old breed

I'm one 'f the old breed. We do things the old-<u>fashioned</u> way. Be-cuz the old-fashioned way is the righ' way. It <u>always</u> works. Y' know, they say you godda go with progress. Well, I've seen a lodda progress 'n' it don' work. Y' know wha' I mean? I always remember when they wanned t' make the canal, for boats. So wha' did they do? Cut all the bends in the river off. An' wha' 'appened? They put concrete in. Well, water will go where it can find itself, 'n' tha's it — you ain' gonna stop water. You're not. I like the old-fashioned way. You godda keep it plain 'n' simple. You haven' godda make life difficul'. 'N' this is wha's happenin' in this world now. Ev'rythink's so hard now.

Well, like these youngsters wha' come out fr'm the river people — oh, they know bugger all! I says to 'm: "Wha' classifies <u>you</u> t' tell <u>me</u> how t' do this river?" I says: "'Ow many years you been on the river?" "Well, we 'aven't." I says: "S' how can you come out here 'n' tell me?" They say: "We look it old maps." I says: "Trouble is, old maps change, but you don' grow up with it. You've got t' be on the river at <u>least</u> ten yurz, be-fore you can turn round 'n' say t' me, 'n' I'll say, yeah you're right, cuz you've done it." I tell 'm: "Don' come 'ere with big ideas off 'f a laptop, cuz it ain' gunna work." Anybody c'n look online, but with river work, you've godda get yer hands dirty. It's doin' it <u>manually</u>, usin' yer brain!

When they done the big project 'ere[127], I w's umming 'n' ahh-ing abou' it, when they first star'-ed. <u>Tha'</u> w's all done on compu'-er. You c'd see how it w's gunna look before it w's done. But actually, it w's a brilliant job — I even told 'm. I w's <u>well</u> impressed with it. It's much better fishing now. So, this is why I say, you've got t' go with the times, with the youngsters. Becuz if you don', you're gunna get left be'-ind. I'd have 'm back 'ere any time.

---

[127] A project by the environmental authorities in 2021—22. Its aim was to redress the balance between the natural, chalk stream river ('the carrier') and the man-made leat. The project resulted in more water flowing through the carrier and less through the leat, as well as giving the leat a more natural, gently-meandering shape.

Winter work

Oh I love win'-er! I like it when it's cold, frosty, snowy. Cuz then, when you go in tha' 'ouse you got y' fire burnin', you got the stew ready — stew 'n' dumplin's — oof!

I've always worked outdoors — it don't worry me. Be-cuz in the win'-er you <u>haff</u> t' sort the river out. Tha's the only time you <u>can</u>. Be-cuz there's no fishin', there's nobody t' stop you doin' it. Well, you godda make sure all the banks are sturdy enough, be-cuz they <u>will</u> wash away. You godda cut the weed in the river, otherwise it dies in there 'n' it smells, 'n' then you start gettin' disease in there. 'N' you've godda cut a bit a weed so there's some openin's f' the fishermen. Nah, it's never worried me. But if you get anybody else t' work 'ere they'll work in the summer but they won' work in the win'-er. Tha's wha' you do: you take the job on, if you work outdoors.

Chilly creatures

There's no' a <u>lot</u> 'f life in the winter. Mostly you see the fox, the deers... not s' much the mu'tjacs. I like the fox best. I like the colour 'f 'im. 'N' they c'n creep up to a rabbit before the rabbit knows it's there. It's crazy!

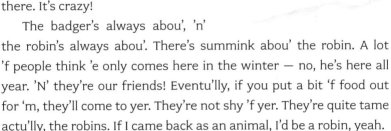

The badger's always abou', 'n' the robin's always abou'. There's summink abou' the robin. A lot 'f people think 'e only comes here in the winter — no, he's here all year. 'N' they're our friends! Eventu'lly, if you put a bit 'f food out for 'm, they'll come to yer. They're not shy 'f yer. They're quite tame actu'lly, the robins. If I came back as an animal, I'd be a robin, yeah.

You see the owl more th'n anythink, but you've got a job t' see 'm when they're in the snow - tha's the only thing. But it's harder f'r 'm t' find food as well, see, in the win'-er. Cuz me 'n' Kyle found one on tha' back road to Everleigh[128] one nigh', when Kyle w's small 'un. 'N' 'e said: "There's summink on the road", 'n' it w's a li'-l white owl. It'd been knocked down, see? He w's dead, 'n' Kyle said: "Wha' sh'll we do with it?" I said: "Le's go up t' the tank crossing[129]", 'n' I said: "We'll bury 'im there". 'N' d' you know wha', 'e <u>never</u> f'got where it is. 'E still knows, t'day. An 'ow you c'n run a owl over, I do not know. Well, people go too <u>faast</u>!

---

[128] Everleigh is a village 10 minutes' drive northeast of Coombe.

[129] One of many crossings for tanks and other military vehicles, when they're out on exercise on Salisbury Plain. The Mill is a peaceful place, but occasionally you can hear a small war going on in the background!

Next generation

I cannot understand why youngsters don' wanna do this job. They all want office jobs, but I'm afraid there ent so many 'f those now.

It's a pity. When I'm gone... You don' see no youngsters comin' up wanna be a river keeper. You see 'm wanna be a game keeper — tha's cuz they wanna shoot things — but not a river keeper, be-cuz it entails tha' winter work. You godda be dedicated. I've 'ad a couple a youngsters in, but in the winter they're not interested. It's a shame. It's a dyin' trade; goin'.

It's like the thatchers; stonemasons. You don' see many youngsters goin' in f' tha'. Cuz it's 'ard work. But river keepin'... Well, it's lovely 'ere on a frosty morning — byoo'-iful innit?! You go into an office 'n you're in four walls all day.

The youngsters, they are doin' it but they 'aven't godda do no physical work, be-cuz they bring in people t' do it. It's not like actually getting in 'n doin' it yerself. They've jus' godda make the plans.

But I would like t' see more girls on the river (ha ha — no, you know wha' I mean — bein' a river keeper), be-cuz I can' see anythink wrong with it. I've always said, if a woman can do the job better than me, crack on, do the job. I've never seen a woman river keeper.

'Ob knobs 'n' jobs

If I w's Prime Minister f' the day, the first thing I would do is I would go back t' the old way 'f a job centre: that people <u>haff</u> t' go an' sign on, instead 'f, they go in once, then the money's sent t' them aafter that, so you don' know if they're doin' other work somewhere else 'n' gettin' the money off the Gov'nm'nt[130] at the same time, see?

An' it should be... if people 've been on the dole for six or nine or twelve months, you offer 'm a job. They don' 'ave that job, they don' get the money. That's how it should be. Sometimes you've godda be tough in this world, but the trouble is, with the Gov'nm'nt [131], they're too soft, 'n' no one will give you a straight aanswer. They won't. They're not worried about me or you. They're don' like the truth — they're <u>frightened</u> 'f us. They just wanna earn the money.

An' when it comes to election, do you ever see 'm? They never come t' the <u>workin'</u> claass people, yer local MPs. They go t' the 'ob knob[132] people with big 'ouses. But we're no diff'r'nt from Joe Bloggs down the road. We'd tell 'm, how it should be told. You aff t' 'ave y' workers, 'n' you aff t' 'ave y' rich people.

Now see wha's 'appened in Parl'am'nt — they're watchin' bluddy porno![133] They're a law 'f their own.

---

[130] T: *Government.*

[131] At the time, it was Boris Johnson's government.

[132] T: *hob knob* (i.e. posh).

[133] Martin was speaking in April 2022, when an MP was caught in the act of looking at pornography on his phone. Something to do with tractors...

Wiltshire's oldest paperboy?

I do the papers on me way t' work. It ain' out me way. I do it f' nuthin'. It all started — Kyle decided 'e'd do a paper round. Then it got tha' Kyle di'n' wanna do it — 'e wouldn' ged up. So I used t' do Haxton 'n' Fittleton[134]. Then Steph took it on but tha' di'n' last long, so I took it back on. I've done Netheravon — especially with what's bin goin' on, with Covit. Be-cuz the council stopped the paper boys fr'm deliverin'. So I used t' do the rounds. I'm comin' t' work so might as well do the papers on me way. Y' know wha' I mean? I mean, tha's wha' I do. I've always done stuff like tha', no problem.

---

[134] Haxton and Fittleton are neighbouring villages, not far from Coombe.

Coming down with Covit

Ooh, Covit[135] w's 'orrible. I couldn' understand why I goddit, be-cuz I work outdoors all the time, but apparently it 'as no priority 'f people — it'll 'ave oo it wants. But I would not wan' anyone t' ged it. I really wouldn': it's horrible. An' the worst thing wuz, I wouldn' shut me eyes it night, cuz I w's frightened I wouldn' wake up in the mornin'. Well, you see it on television. It's that word: until you've goddit, you don' think nuthin' of it. If someb'dy said to you: "Positive — you've got Covit," bang! You'd think: "Shit!"

I 'ad real, vile headaches — ah! I said t' the NHS woman — be-cuz they used t' ring twice a day to moniter yer — I said, if I could've cut my 'ead off, I would. Tha's how bad it w's, 'n' I still gets 'm now 'n' again. 'N' then, I'd take Cokey for a walk across the field, 'n' all 'f a sudden yer legs jus' go like jelly 'n' you aff t' stop.

I slept, 'n' tha's all you wanna do is sleep. But the most important thing you've godda do, even if you don' want to, is eat, 'an' this is wha' I did. That's the only way t' fight it[136].

I w's lucky not t' aff t' go t' 'ospital. I think a lot 'f it is be-cuz I've worked outdoors all me life. If I'd worked in an office it could've been a diff'r'nt situation altogether.

I w's brought up in the country, 'n' we've got the attitude that you just godda get on with life. But now, ev'ry day I make it a good day. Tha's the way you've godda look ad it now. Until you've 'ad it, people jus' laaf about it. Well, we're livin' in a diff'r'nt world now. It might never go away, like the flu in winter, so make the best 'f life while you can, 'n' try 'n' lead a normal life.

---

[135] T: *Covid*. Martin had Covid in early 2021.

[136] Disclaimer: this is Martin's view, not necessarily medical advice, but it seems to have worked for him.

Proud dad

In life I'm most proud 'f my kids, I think — yep, my kids.

I've 'ad Steph since she w's five, 'n' she done well, be-cuz when she w's younger, she w's a li'l shit! She used t' be in a girl gang, 'n' she w's the 'ead girl, 'n' she used t' get in trouble <u>all</u> the time. 'N' then when they star'-ed t' drink, I used t' 'ave t' go t' Salz'b'ry police station on a Sund'y t' ged 'er out. I said to 'er one day: "You got two choices 'ere: you eether be'-ave or you c'n go 'n' live with yer mum." 'N' she's still 'ere. After tha' day she never drinks no more. And she changed from tha' day onwards.

She worked in the shop in Netheravon[137], 'n' then fr'm there she went t' Britax[138], 'n' she's been there ever since — she loves it. You caan' <u>stop</u> 'er goin' t' work! She loves 'er work,

---

[137] Netheravon is another nearby village.

[138] Britax Römer — A company that manufactures car seats for children/babies, pushchairs and accessories. The factory has now moved its operations to Germany, so Steph has moved on.

'n' it's the <u>people</u> 's well — the Polish people; all the women there: they make 'er welcome. Cuz Steph'nie's a bit shy, believe it or not — she doesn't mingle with a lodda people — but she <u>does</u> like those, 'n' tha's why she gets on well. She's a supervisor now.

There's two things I'm proud 'f Kyle. One is when 'e told me 'e w's gay, 'n' 'e w's <u>frightened</u> t' death. 'E told <u>ev'rybody</u> else, 'n' 'e came 'ome, an' 'e said: "Dad, can I talk to yer?" I said: "Yeah, course you can." 'N' 'e sat down 'n' 'e said: "Dad, I'm gay." I said: "So?" I said: "End 'f the day, you're my son. Whatever in life, I'm there be-'ind yer." Best day 'f my life w's when 'e got married t' Aaron, best day 'f my life. Cuz I <u>never</u> thought I'd see 'im get married.

The other one w's when 'e star'-ed working with autism children. Cuz I'd <u>never</u> believe it if I di'n' see it, tha' tha's wha' he wanned t' do. Cuz 'e worked in the shop, 'n' it w's a good thing, be-cuz I kept on t' him: "Ged a job — yer not livin' 'ere f' nuthin'!" 'n' 'e got the job, 'n' then a woman come in one day who w's the boss 'f autism children it a school. An' she'd hear'-d that 'e'd been lookin' after a couple 'f autism children, baby-sittin' — cuz 'e used t' do a lodda tha' — an' he got right into it, 'n' 'e's never looked back.

He's another one wha' <u>loves</u> his job. You caan' stop him goin' t' work, see? Or me. It's in the family. Y' know, 'e's makin' summink 'f 'is life. 'E's got a chance to do it 'n' 'e's doin' it — where we di'n' at our age. 'E's studyin', be-cuz 'e wants t' go t' university an' study the brain 'f autism children. Be-cuz I di'n' realise there's so many diff'r'nt sorts 'f autism. Never knew tha'! 'E knows wha' 'e wants in life 'n' tha's good. Tha's more than a lot 'f 'm do.

Ageing gracefully(ish)

I've mellowed over the yurz. But Steph an' my boy said t' me: "You piss yer pants, you're in a 'ome[139]." Yeah, unbelievable!

---

[139] T: *You'll be in a retirement home.*

No regrets

Do I 'ave any regrets? Nah, not really. Always wanned a work on a farm, always wanned a be outside. Don' wan' a lot out 'f life — y' know, roof over me 'ead, food in the pantry, 'n' payin' me rent. I jus' wan' a simple life — tha's all I ever wanned. I don't want f' nuthink really. Be-cuz, it's jus' greed when y' do.

Any other business

There's not much more I c'n say — not livin' round 'ere, with wha' I used t' get up to. I'd get shot. Unbelievable!

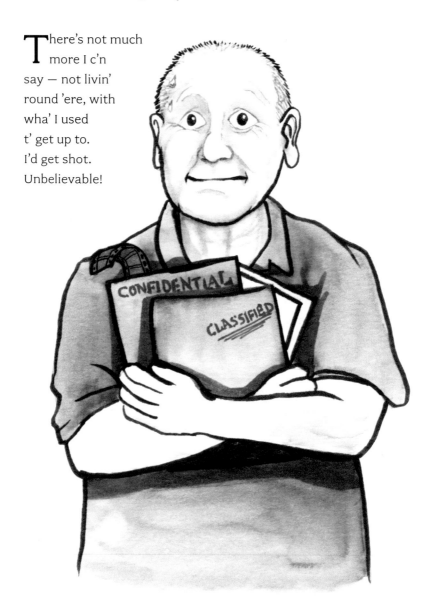

Postscript - Martin's art

Martin is multi-talented and will turn his hand to anything. Once, he mentioned to me that he can draw. I asked him what kind of things, and he said: "All sorts, like Chinese costumes." I must admit that this was a surprise to me, as I've only ever known him doing big, physical work and not fine detail, but I was impressed. However, it was said in passing, so I didn't think much more about it.

It was only when we were looking through Martin's old photos for this book that I was reminded of his art and realised that he really can draw! He showed me some faded photos from the 1970s, in which he'd captured some of his illustrations of nature and life, and some calligraphy that he'd done. I was stunned. Among other things, he had drawn delicate, colourful birds and flowers, to a standard that could have offered him an alternative career, or at least a lucrative side job. On seeing these I had to remind myself never to judge a book by its cover.

If you'd like to see some of Martin's old illustrations (faded but restored as much as possible), they can be found on my website (**victoriawalshwrites.com**) and at **vicwalshwrites** on Facebook, Instagram and Twitter.

Acknowledgements

This book has been a team effort, and of course the person most worth thanking is **Martin Aris** himself. I really couldn't have done it without him! He was very generous in telling me his story, and very patient along the way.

As well as Martin, I'd like to thank:

- **Chalk Stream Books** (chalkstreambooks.com), for being such a great local publisher;
- **Alex Crump** (alexcrumpillustration.com), for his beautiful illustrations, which really bring Martin's story to life;
- **Simon Cooper** (fishingbreaks.co.uk), for the well-crafted and heartfelt foreword;
- **Simon Bragg**, my partner, for being so supportive and reviewing several drafts;
- **Anne Heath**, for various photos for the book and its marketing;
- **Jacky Freer**, an ex colleague and communication specialist who kindly reviewed the book;
- **Rob Phayre** (robphayre.com), an ex colleague and author who gave me lots of helpful advice;
- **Sophie Coulthard**, a friend and author (ditto);
- **Angie Langley** (jenniferbrownsjourney.co.uk), another helpful author, with the same publisher;
- **Bianca Raluca** (Snappy Snaps Farringdon, London), for help with the photos;
- **Neil Rhodes** (image-restore.co.uk), for specialist restoration of some damaged photos; and
- **John Cheyne** (anglingtrust.net) for being willing to partner with the book, in spite of the references to poaching!

About the author

Victoria Walsh is a writer with a passion for people stories, community and the countryside.

A community relations professional and linguist by background, Victoria has always enjoyed writing, and engaging with people from all walks of life.

Originally a city girl, Victoria moved to Wiltshire in 2015, fell in love with the countryside and rediscovered her creative side.

It was there too that she met Martin Aris, river keeper for the stretch of the River Avon that runs past her house, and now the unforgettable subject of *Unbelievable! A Working Country Life*.

About the illustrator

Alex Crump lives in the Wiltshire countryside with his young family, a very affectionate elderly cat and a huge ginger cat. He can often be found in his studio, creating work in a myriad of media, from paint and pencil to charcoal and Photoshop.

Alex's past careers as a teacher and zookeeper, as well as other current side-lines of storyteller and charity/museum Educator, allow him to bring plenty of ideas to the work he produces.

Find out more at alexcrumpillustration.com.

Martin and more

There's much more to Martin than I've been able to capture in the book, and there's more to me as a writer, too! For more Martin-related stories, pictures and videos, as well as for my more general blog (see my website) with other stories about people, community and the countryside, please visit the following sites:

- **Website**: victoriawalshwrites.com;
- **Facebook**: facebook.com/vicwalshwrites;
- **Instagram**: instagram.com/vicwalshwrites; and
- **Twitter**: twitter.com/vicwalshwrites.

I'd love you to join my **mailing list**, which will provide more of the above, as well as some special offers. To join, please either use the contact form on my website or email me at **victoriawalsh.info@gmail.com**. You can unsubscribe at any time.

Finally, I'd be very grateful for book **reviews**, through my website, social media, email, or where the book is sold online.